KWB7

STRIP QUILTING PROJECTS 2

Projects from the "Strip Quilting 2" series as shown on PBS-TV stations

by

Kaye Wood

Cover quilt: Denim scraps used to make Rocky Road & Courthouse Steps quilts to cover waste baskets.

ISBN No: 0-944588-12-3

4949 Rau Rd.
West Branch, MI 48661

A SPECIAL THANK YOU
TO THE SPONSORS
OF MY
SECOND TELEVISION SERIES
"STRIP QUILTING 2"

VIKING SEWING MACHINE CO.
11750 Berea Road
Cleveland, OH 44111
Manufacturers of
VIKING SEWING MACHINES and HUSKYLOCK SERGERS

and

HOBBS BONDED FIBERS
P.O. Box 151
Groesbeck, TX 76642
Manufacturers of
POLY-DOWN batting, fiberfill, THERMORE & Pillow Inserts

AND THANK YOU TO:

Concord Fabrics for most of the fabric used
Jane Ehinger of West Branch, MI for sharing her flying geese design
and to
Marty Lawrence of Flint, MI for her special hand-dyed fabrics
Information on her hand-dyed fabrics is available
by writing to:
Marty Lawrence
P.O. Box 4602
Flint, MI 48504

PHOTOGRAPHY BY: JUDY JOHANNES PHOTOGRAPHY
West Branch, MI

Television series "Strip Quilting" produced by:
David Larson Productions
P.O. Box 26497
Milwaukee, WI 53226

TABLE OF CONTENTS

CHAPTER 1: INTRODUCTION

CHAPTER 2: PROJECTS

CHAPTER 3: FINISHING TECHNIQUES

SEMINARS & WORKSHOPS
by
KAYE WOOD
4949 Rau Road
West Branch, MI 48661
517-345-3028

NEW TECHNIQUES for
FAST, EASY and ACCURATE MACHINE STRIP PIECING--
ALL WITHOUT TEMPLATES
developed by Kaye Wood

SEMINARS (Lecture /Demonstration /Trunk Show)

*3 different 2-hour seminars -- a total of 6 hours
*quick tips and ideas for machine patchwork
*over 150 step-by-step samples & finished quilts
*good for large or small groups
*informative and entertaining

1. CREATIVE PATCHWORK
   Fast methods for traditional patchwork
   Combining and creating new patterns
   Ideas taken from several of Kaye's books

2. LOG CABIN VARIATIONS
   Fast strip piecing of the basic Log Cabin
   Reversible quilts
   Triangles & diamonds

3. STARMAKERS
   New & easier ways to make stars,
   Tumbling blocks, Spiderwebs & Diamonds

SIT-AND-SEW WORKSHOPS

*Several different 6-hour workshops
*Limited to 30 students -- sewing machines needed
*Learn Kaye's techniques for accurate piecing

1. LOG CABIN DIAMONDS
2. LOG CABIN TRIANGLES
3. REVERSIBLE QUILTS
4. BASIC LOG CABIN
5. STRING STAR VARIATIONS--Jane's Morning Star
6. SMALL LONE STAR
7. BISCUIT or PUFF QUILTS

CHAPTER 1:

INTRODUCTION

to
"STRIP QUILTING PROJECTS, Volume 2"

These projects are all included in my second television series, "STRIP QUILTING 2".

Strip piecing and accurate angles --
that makes the STRIP LIKE A PRO Program special and unique.

The STRIP LIKE A PRO Program is made up of all of my books, tools, and videos.

BOOKS---go step-by-step through the techniques for easy and accurate strip piecing.

STARMAKER TOOLS--- for accurate angles.

VIDEOS---to visualize the steps for more accurate piecing and to show you a wide range of color & design possibilities.

When you combine STRIP PIECING with the STARMAKER tools,
you insure accurate angles:

STARMAKER 5---
18 degree angle for 20-piece Dresden Plates & 5-piece fans
72 degree angle for 5-pointed designs

STARMAKER 6---
60 degree angle for 6-pointed designs

STARMAKER 8---
22-1/2 degree angle for 16-piece Dresden Plates & 4-piece fans
45 degree angle for 8-pointed designs
90 degree angle for square & rectangles

SUPPLIES NEEDED

The supplies which will make your STRIP PIECING PROJECTS easier and more accurate are:

- The Starmaker 5 tool
- The Starmaker 6 tool
- The Starmaker 8 tool
- A heavy plastic ruler, such as the Quickline or the O'Lipfa
- The Olfa rotary cutter & mat
- Iron
- Magnetic seam guide
- Double-faced basting tape
- The View-A-Strip

ACCURACY -- CUTTING, SEWING, PRESSING

MEASURING

Always use the same ruler to cut the width of your strips within any one project. Rulers are not always the same; and changing from one ruler to another can result in strips that are not cut the same width. By using the same ruler, your measurements will be more accurate.

CUTTING THE STRIPS

All of the designs in this book are made with strips of fabric. Most strips are cut across the width of the fabric (44"/45"), from selvedge edge to selvedge edge.

Fabrics with a lengthwise design can be more effective when the strips are cut lengthwise. Fabrics such as stripes, or the poly-cotton moires I like to use, will give you a completely different look depending on whether they are cut across the width or lengthwise. Use the VIEW-A-STRIP tool to help you decide which way will be more effective.

To cut strips with the rotary cutter:

Fold the fabric in half with selvedge edges together.

Lay the folded fabric on the rotary cutter mat.
(Be sure the fabric lays flat, even if the cut or torn edges are not together.)
The fold of the fabric should be lined up with one edge of the mat or a grid line on the mat.

Cut the fabric perpendicular to the fold to straighten one edge, using the rotary cutter and a heavy plastic ruler, such as the Quickline Ruler or the O'Lipfa ruler.

Fold the fabric once more by bring the folded edge to the selvedge edge--the fabric will now be in 4 layers; the shorter length will be easier to cut without the ruler slipping.

Cut the rest of the strips needed. Use the lines on the ruler to cut accurate strips, e.g., to cut 1 1/2" wide strips, place the 1 1/2" line on the ruler at the cut edge of the fabric. Pull the rotary cutter along the edge of the ruler.

SEWING ACCURATELY

Sewing accurately is very important. You might want to try a magnetic seam guide on your machine to help you line up the strips of fabric as you sew. It really does make a difference. But the magnetic seam guide can cause problems with the computer in other brands of computer sewing machines; so check with the manufacturer of your machine. It causes no problems with my Viking.

Usually in patchwork 1/4" seam allowances are used. With the techniques in my books, any seam allowance will work, but you must be consistent.

Chain Stitch- stitching from one piece of fabric directly on to the next without cutting thread. In strip piecing, cut combinations are usually sewn to long strips of fabric; then the long strips are cut. Cut combinations are also sewn to other cut combinations one right after the other.

Combination Strips -- two or more strips of fabric sewn together lengthwise.

Cut Combinations -- pieces cut from the combination strip. They can be squares, rectangles, triangles or diamonds.

Serging Machine or Serger- sews, overcasts and trims the seam allowance all at the same time. Most of the projects in this book can be done on either the sewing machine or serger. Serging patchwork is faster and can be just as accurate. Pressing seam allowances is faster and easier because the seams are already overcast together. Your patchwork will also have neater and flatter seam allowances.

MATCHING SEAMLINES WITHOUT PINNING

There are several methods which I use to match seamlines without pinning:

Double-faced basting tape--for matching points. The tape with its paper or plastic backing is placed within the seam allowance on the right side of the fabric. Press in place with your fingers. Remove the paper backing. Lay the second piece of fabric, right sides together, on top of the taped fabric. Check on the right sides to make sure the seam lines or points match perfectly. Then finger press the two layers of fabric together. Sew on the seam line. Remove the basting tape. Press the seam allowances.

Finger Pinning - holding seam allowances together with fingers as they start to feed through the sewing machine.

If the seam allowances go in opposite directions, try to sew them together with the top seam allowance laying toward the needle and away from you. The feed dogs on your machine will push the top layer of fabric into the seam on the bottom fabric. This is the easiest seam line to match.

If the top seam allowance lays away from the needle and toward you, you will have to hold the seam lines together firmly as you sew toward them.

PRESSING ACCURATELY

Pressing correctly is important in all kinds of patchwork; it becomes even more important when you work with angles in your designs.

Seam allowances are usually pressed to one side in patchwork; BUT before pressing the seam allowances toward one side, press the seamline in the position it was sewn. This will help to keep the stitches locked in the center of the fabric. It will also restore any stretching that occurs when sewing bias cut fabric.

Accurate pressing is insured by:

1. pressing with the grain of the fabric.
2. pressing from the right side of the fabric.
3. no steam

Pressing with the grain. Pressing (an up and down motion with the iron) is much different than ironing (a side to side gliding motion). Ironing can stretch fabric if it goes along the crosswise grain of the fabric, e.g., moving the iron along the length of the **strip.**

Pressing from the right side of the fabric --Pressing from the wrong side can result in pleats forming at the seamline. To press from the right side of the fabric, follow these directions:

1. Each time a new strip is added, lay the patchwork on the ironing board; the new strip will be wrong side up, the rest of the quilt block will be right side up.
2. Use the side of the iron to press the new strip away from the finished piece. The seam allowance will lay toward the new strip.

No Steam -- Steam is useful in clothing construction to put shaping into the pieces of a garment. Using steam in strip piecing can cause the strips of fabric to stretch.

LOG CABIN QUILTS

Log Cabin designs are traditionally associated with prairie or frontier life. The names of the many different designs--
Barn Raising, Fields & Furrows, Court House Steps, Straight Furrows, Streak of Lightning, etc.--reflect the life of rural America.

These designs are formed by the positioning of the light and dark sides of the blocks, as they are joined together.

And the **color of the fabric** traditionally used in Log Cabin designs also represents life on the frontier.
If the center square in each block is red or orange, it represents the center of their Log Cabin home--the fire in the fireplace.
If the center square is gold, it represents the sun.
If the center square is yellow, it represents the lantern hung in the window so the men could find their way back from the fields after dark.

The fabrics used for the strips (logs) to build the Log Cabin are usually separated into lights and darks.
If the center is red for the fire,
the light colored strips represent the light from the fireplace;
while the dark strips represent the shadows cast from the fire.
If the center is gold for the sun, the light strips are the daylight;
the dark strips are the night.
Another story is that if the center is gold for the sun,
the light strips are the highlights of a person's life, such as births; the dark strips then represent the tragedies of life, such as death.

All the light colored strips can be cut from the same light fabric, or a different light colored fabric can be used for each strip (e.g., a light, medium and a dark). The same is true for the dark colored strips.

BASIC INSTRUCTIONS FOR LOG CABIN QUILTS

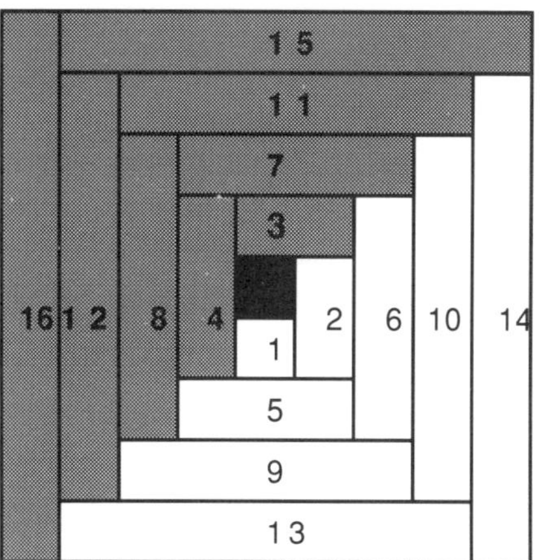

All projects start with a CENTER (C) piece;

Strips (from #1 to #16) are added to all four sides counterclockwise, or in some designs, to just two sides.
Some of the projects will only have 4 strips added; some 16 strips.
Some projects are made from square blocks (known as the Basic Log Cabin);
Some are squares that are off-centered;
Some are diamonds, triangles and even a Pineapple.
But all of them are called Log Cabins because of the way they are constructed and strip pieced.

C, shown in black, is the center of the block; it is usually a contrasting color.

Strips #1 & #2	-	usually light colored; usually from the same fabric.				
Strips #3 & #4	-	"	dark	"	"	"
Strips #5 & #6	-	"	light	"	"	"
Strips #7 & #8	-	"	dark	"	"	"
Strips #9
-	"	light	"	"	"
Strips #11	-	"	dark	"	"	"
Strips #13	-	"	light	"	"	"
Strips #15	-	"	dark	"	"	"

Any variations in the following steps are given in the individual projects.

Step 1: Cut the strips needed following the instructions for each project.
Sew the center (C) strip to the #1 strip.
You now have a combination strip, made up of 2 strips.
Press the seam allowance toward the #1 strip and away from the Center (C) strip.
(see pressing instructions)

All seam allowances in every Log Cabin will always be pressed away from the Center.

Step 2: Cut the combination strip into pieces as wide as the Center strip,
(e.g. if the Center strip is 2", cut this combination strip every 2").

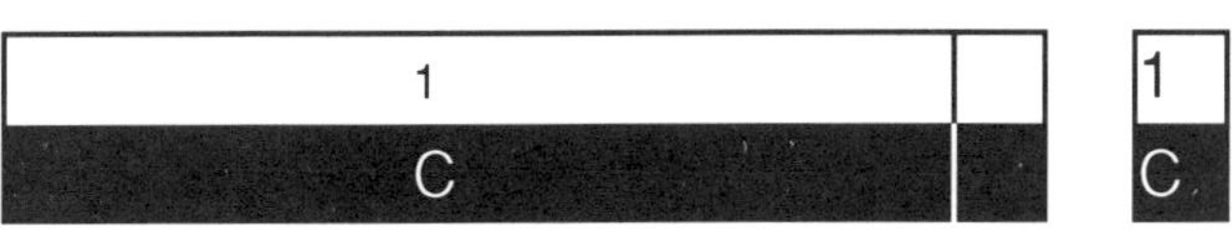

This is the only time you will need to do any measuring during the construction of the blocks.
Cut one piece for each of the blocks in your design.

Step 3: Sew these pieces (blocks) to a #2 strip.
Lay the pieces one right after the other on the strip, right sides together.
The center (C) square is toward you as you sew; the #1 piece is toward the machine, or away from you.
The seam allowance lays toward the machine, so hold it down as you sew it..
Your pieces should line up perfectly on the strip.
If the pieces are narrower or wider that the #2 strip, you need to go back to Step 2 and recut them.

Press the seam allowances away from the center strip.

2
1
C
1
C
1
C
2

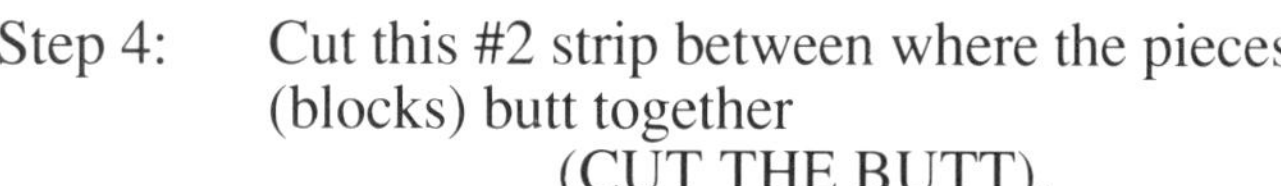

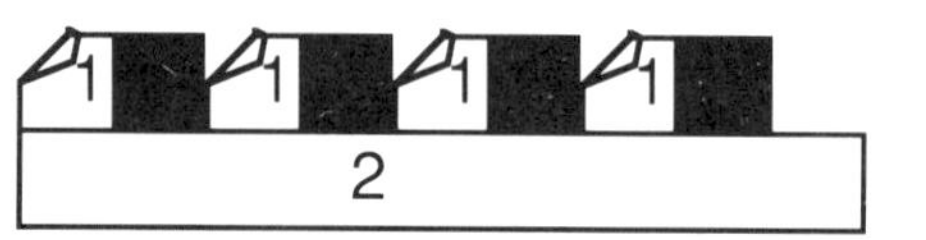

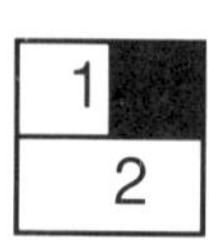

Step 4: Cut this #2 strip between where the pieces (blocks) butt together
(CUT THE BUTT).

CAUTION: Be sure to only cut the #2 strip, and not the blocks.

Step 5: Sew these pieces (blocks) to a #3 strip.
Lay the pieces on the strip, right sides together.
The pieces should butt together, but not overlap.
The center square is toward you as you sew.
The #2 piece is toward the machine, or away from you.
The seam allowance lays toward the machine.

Press the seam allowances away from the Center and toward the new strip.

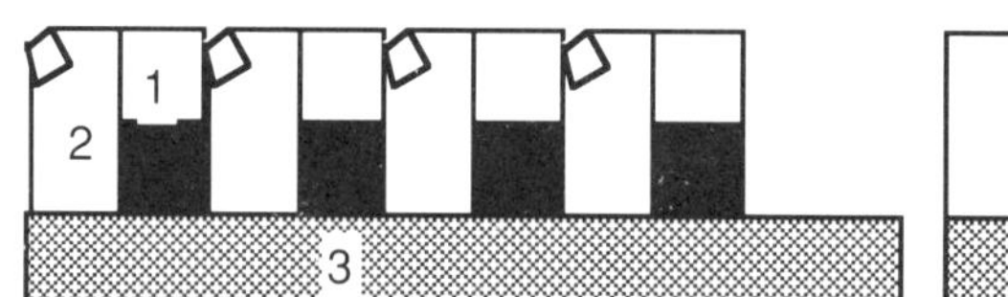

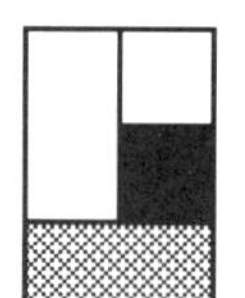

Step 6: Cut the #3 strip in between the pieces (blocks).

Step 7: Sew these blocks to the #4 strip.
The last strip added to the block will always be away from you as you are sewing the blocks to a new strip.
The first seam allowance of the quilt block will lay toward the machine as you sew; The second seam allowance will lay toward you.

Press the seam allowances toward the new strip and away from the center.

Step 8: Cut the #4 strip in between the quilt blocks.

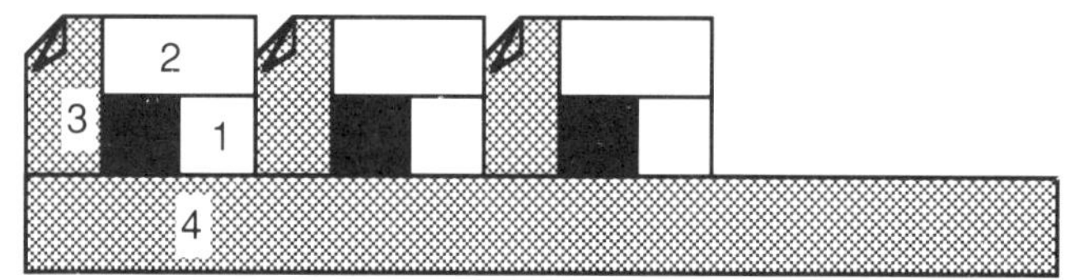

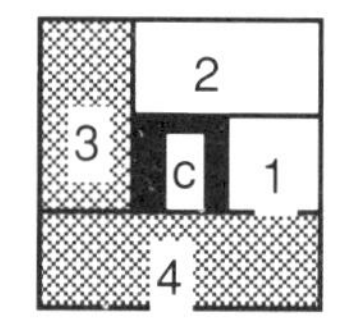

Step 9: Continue adding strips to the quilt blocks until your blocks are finished, following the directions in the individual projects.

DON'T SEW THE STRIPS TOGETHER TO MAKE THEM LONGER.
When your new strip isn't long enough for all the blocks, just sew as many as possible to a strip; sew the rest of the blocks to one or more other strips, as necessary.

CHAPTER 2: PROJECTS

PROJECT 1: LOG CABIN PLACEMAT
(Quilt-As-You-Go)

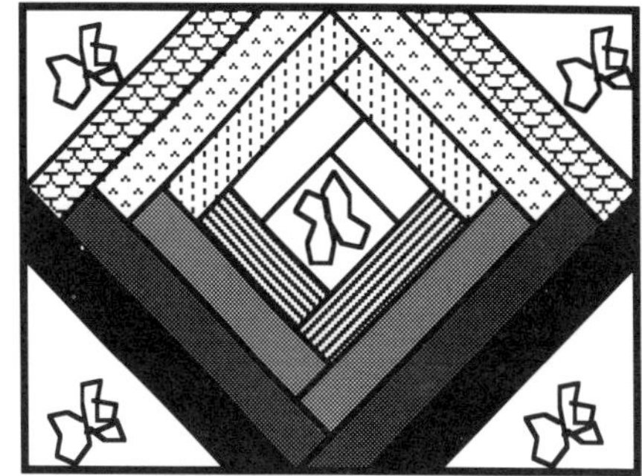

A Log Cabin square, placed on point, makes an attractive placemat. Mine is done in blues & purples; the center and outside corners are from a large floral print. This placemat is a quilt-as-you-go project, which means strips are added to the center, backing and fleece all at the same time.

Finished size: 12" x 16"

The bobbin thread will show on the back, so be sure it matches the backing fabric.

Fabric needed:

center (C) & outside corners		6" x 24"
lightest blue	(#1 & 2)	2" x 7"
2nd blue fabric	(#5 & 6)	2" x 13"
3rd blue fabric	(#9 & 10)	2" x 18"
darkest blue	(#13 & 14)	2" x 20"
lightest purple	(#3 & 4)	2" x 10"
2nd purple	(#7 & 8)	2" x 15"
3rd purple	(#11 & 12)	2" x 20"
darkest purple	(#15 & 16)	2" x 22"
backing fabric		12" x 16"
fleece or Thermore		12" x16"
binding	2 strips	2-1/2" x 44/45"

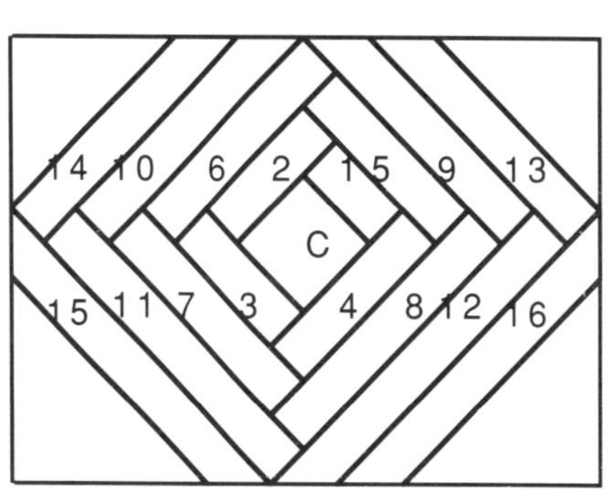

12" x 16"

Step 1: Mark center lines on fleece from top to bottom and side to side.
Layer the backing (right side down) and the fleece; baste zigzag these two layers together around all 4 edges.

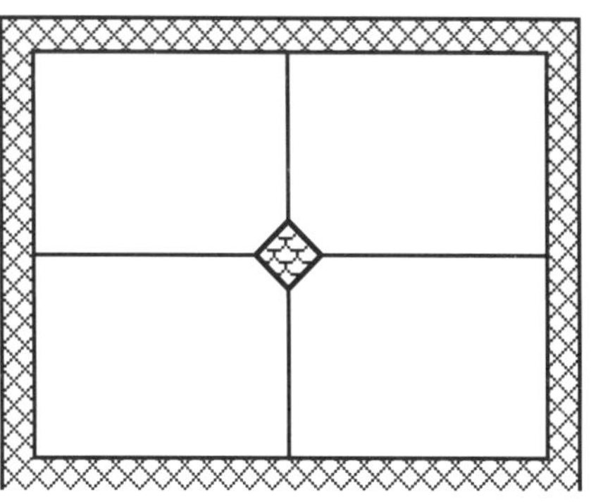

Step 2: Cut out a 2-1/2" x 2-1/2" Center (C)
Center it on-point on the fleece using the marked lines on the fleece as a centering guide.
Pin in place.

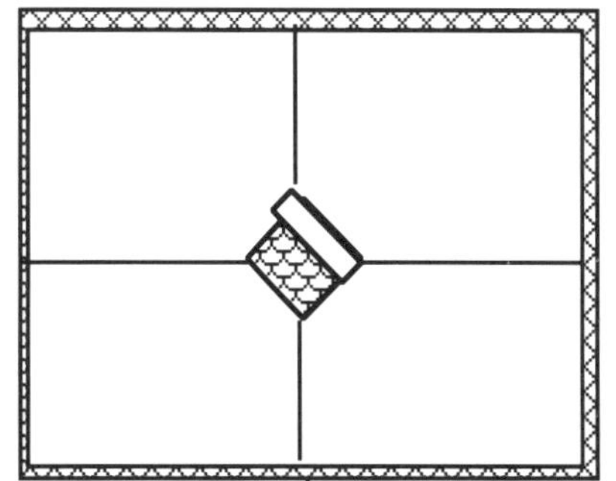

Step 3: Sew the #1 strip, right sides down, on top of and even with the upper right side of the center piece, as shown.
Just sew it the length of the C piece.
Trim the #1 strip even with the C piece.
Open out the strip and pin in place.

Step 4: Sew the #2 strip, right sides down, on top of and even with the upper left side of the C and #1 piece.
Just sew it the length of the C and #1 piece.

Trim the #2 strip even with the C and the #1 piece.
Open out the strip and pin in place.

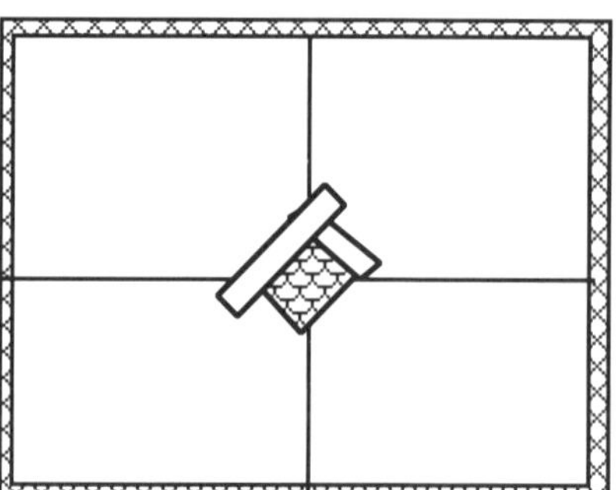

Step 5: Sew the #3 strip, right sides down, even with the lower left side of the C and #2 piece.
Just sew the length of the C & #2 piece and trim.

Open out the strip and pin in place.

Step 6: Sew the #4 strip, right sides down, even with the lower right side of the C and #3 piece.
Sew and trim even with the C and #3 piece.
Open out the strip and pin in place.

Step 7: Continue adding strips counter-clockwise around the center.
Trim any strips that extend beyond the backing & fleece.

Step 8: After all the 2" strips are added, use the 6" strip to finish each corner.
Trim to the backing & fleece size.

Add a binding (see the finishing chapter) and your placemat is finished and, best of all, it's already quilted.

On the back of the placemat, remove the stitches that extend beyond each stitching line back to the stitching line for neater quilting lines.

For other quilt-as-you-go projects, see "Quilt Like A Pro" by Kaye Wood.

PROJECT 2: WOVEN STRIPES WALLHANGING

(Using Stripes for an interesting woven effect)

Stripes are an easy way to color coordinate your projects. You can make each strip look like a different fabric by using different parts of the stripe. Stripes are usually cut lengthwise with a design centered in the middle of the strip. However, there are some stripes that are just as interesting cut across the width of the fabric.

To get the woven look to your wall hanging, the last two striped fabrics (#8 & #9) you sew to each of the 16 blocks must have a definite stripe as part of the design.

Cut stripes one layer of fabric at a time, instead of several layers, so your cutting lines follow the stripe.

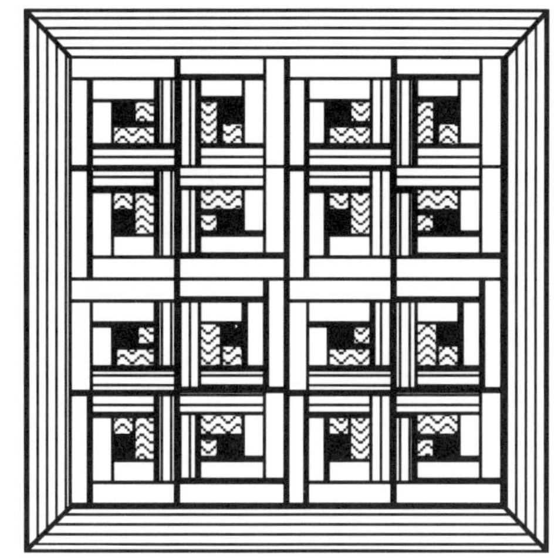

Finished size: 35" x 35"

I cut my striped fabric lengthwise into 2" strips. To center the stripe, place a ruler with the 1" line directly on the middle of the striped design. But, you may have a stripe that will look better cut into wider or narrower strips. Let your fabric dictate the width strip you use. Or, you might want to cut some stripes lengthwise and some across the width for a completely different look.

I used just one striped fabric for my dark color--but each strip looks like a different fabric. For my light fabric, I used all the same tie-dyed fabric.

So I only used 3 fabrics for this piece--

the small center red squares, the striped fabric, and the hand-dyed fabric.

The borders are also made from the striped fabric.

IF YOU PREFER NOT TO USE A STRIPED FABRIC OR TIE-DYED FABRIC, choose two light fabrics and two dark fabrics--and follow the Basic Instructions for Log Cabin Quilts.

Fabric Needed for 16 blocks:

center squares -	1 strip 2" x 34"
striped fabric -	2-3 yards should be enough for squares and borders (depending on the number of strips you choose to use from the fabric, and how much waste there is in between strips)
tie-dyed fabric -	3/4 yard
borders -	4 strips 5" x 40"
batting-	37" x 37"
backing -	37" x 37"
binding -	4 strips 1-1/4" x 40"

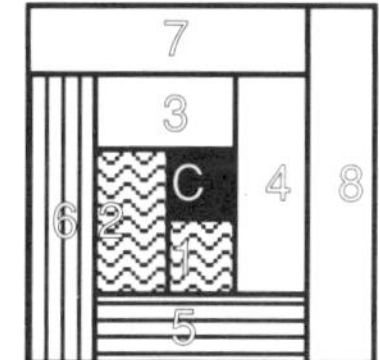

Step 1: Follow the basic instructions for Log Cabin quilts, using the center (C) plus 8 strips (#1-#8). Cut all strips 2".

Step 2: Sew your completed blocks into rows as shown.
Match your seamlines carefully. If necessary, use pins.
Press the seam allowances of the rows in alternating directions, for easier piecing.

Step 3: Sew the rows together. matching seamlines. Press.

Step 4: Add your striped borders.
(Directions for square and mitered borders are in the Finishing Chapter.)

Step 5: Finish your quilt (see Finishing Chapter)
Layer your quilt.

Quilt it--

in the ditch between dark and light fabrics
or, diagonally through corners of the blocks
or, in circles through corners of strips.

Bind it with a faced binding.
Hang it--with a sleeve or hang tabs

For other Log Cabin square designs, see the book, "Quilt Like A Pro" or the video, "Basic Log Cabin"--by Kaye Wood

PROJECT 3: THUNDERBIRD WALLHANGING

(16 Log Cabin Blocks)

16 blocks are needed for this wallhanging. The strips will be cut into 2 different widths, which makes the center square of each block off-center; this makes your design flow across the project and is called a Thunderbird in Indian lore.

Finished size: 20" x 20"

Fabric Needed:

Centers (C)	1 strip	1-1/2" x 26"
1st light fabric (#1&2) --	2 strips	1-1/2" x 44/45"
2nd light fabric (#5&6) --	3 strips	1-1/2" x 44/45"
3rd light fabric (#9&10) --	4 strips	1-1/2" x 44/45"
1st dark fabric (#3&4) --	2 strips	1" x 44/45"
2nd dark fabric (#7&8) --	3 strips	1" x 44/45"
3rd dark fabric (#11&12) --	4 strips	1" x 44/45"
Borders -	2 strips	1-1/2" x 44/45"
Backing -	21" x 21"	
Batting -	21" x 21"	
Binding & hang tabs --	3 strips	2" x 44/45"

Step 1: Follow the basic instructions for Log Cabin quilts. Even though your strips are cut different widths, the sewing, pressing, & cutting techniques are the same.

Row 1 & 2

Step 2: Sew your quilt blocks into rows, as shown.

Row 3 & 4

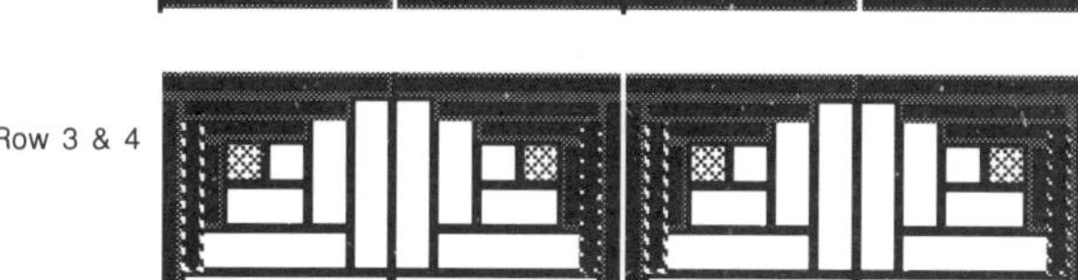

Step 3: Cut a 2" x 20" strip for hanging tabs. Fold into thirds using iron and pin (see Finishing Chapter) Top stitch close to both long edges. Cut the tab strip into 4 equal pieces.

Step 4: Fold the binding strip in half lengthwise using an iron and pin (see Finishing Chapter). Sew the binding to the right side of the wallhanging, mitering the corners.

Step 5: Place the 4 tabs evenly on the back side of the wallhanging, with both raw edges even with the top. Machine stitch in place.

Step 6: Bring the folded edge of the binding to the back, mitering the corners; hand stitch in place. Hang your quilt with a painted or stained dowel rod through the hang tabs.

Other Log Cabin Quilt designs can be found in the book,"Quilt Like A Pro" by Kaye Wood and on her video, "Basic Log Cabin."

PROJECT 4: COURT HOUSE STEPS QUILT

(35 Log Cabin quilt blocks)

This quilt will fit either a twin bed (mattress size 39"x75") as a bed spread or a full size bed (mattress size 54"x75") as a throw. But it's also easy to add another row to make it larger.

Denim & red bandana prints are a natural for that teenager or college student. My 5 children all had a denim quilt--much more practical for their growing-up years than a quilt made from traditional quilting fabrics. My denim quilts are scrap quilts made from blue jeans, after the knees and the seats were finally worn too thin to be patched any more, with all of the wonderful variations and shades of blue. You might call them memory quilts--for all of the blue jeans used were worn by my children as they were growing up. They can even spot their favorite pair in the quilts, and like to remember those years.

Finished size: 68" x 96"

If you have a serger, try it on this quilt--it will keep all of those edges from ravelling.

Fabrics needed:

blue jeans	approximately 4 yds.
cut strips as long as possible and 2" wide	
Strips can be cut both the length & width of the jean leg.	
Cut across the side seam occasionally for added interest.	
red bandana prints	approximately 3 yards
backing (I used red bandana print)	5-1/2 yards
batting:	70" x 100"

11
7
3
9 5 1 C 2 6 10
4
8
12

Denim is used for:

- Center (C) strip
- Strips #3 & 4
- Strips #7 & 8
- Strips #11 & 12

Red bandana print is used for:

- Strips #1 & 2
- Strips #5 & 6
- Strips #9 & 10

Step 1: Cut fabrics into 2" wide strips.
Sew a red strip (#1 & 2) to each side of a denim strip (C).

Step 2: Press seam allowances away from the C strip; toward the red strips.

Step 3: Cut this combination strip into 2" pieces.

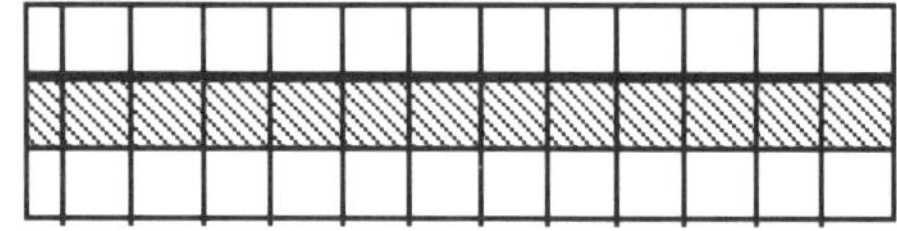

1
C
2

You will need 35 of these 2" pieces--one for each of the 35 blocks.

Step 4: Sew these pieces to a denim (#3) strip, right sides together.
Sew with one red piece toward the machine and one red piece toward you.
Sew as many as possible to each strip.

Step 5: Trim the #3 denim strip even with the pieces.

Step 6: Sew a denim (#4) strip to the other side of each of these pieces.
Sew with one red piece toward the machine; the other red piece toward you.
Trim the denim strip even with the pieces (blocks).
Press seam allowances toward the denim strips.

Step 7: Sew these pieces (blocks) one right after the other, right sides together, to a red strip (#5).

Remember: The red strips will always be sewn to both sides of the quilt block; the denim strips will be sewn to the top and bottom of the block.

Cut the #5 red strip in between the pieces (blocks).
Sew the opposite side of the block to a #6 red strip.
Cut the #6 red strip even with each block.
Press seam allowances toward the #4 strips.

Step 8: Continue adding denim strips to the top and bottom; red strips to both sides. Your block is finished when you have 4 strips on each side of the center square.

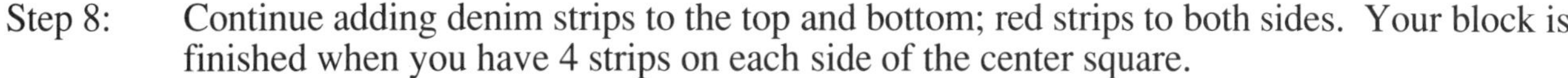

Step 9: Sew 5 blocks together into each row with the denim at the top and bottom, the red at the sides.

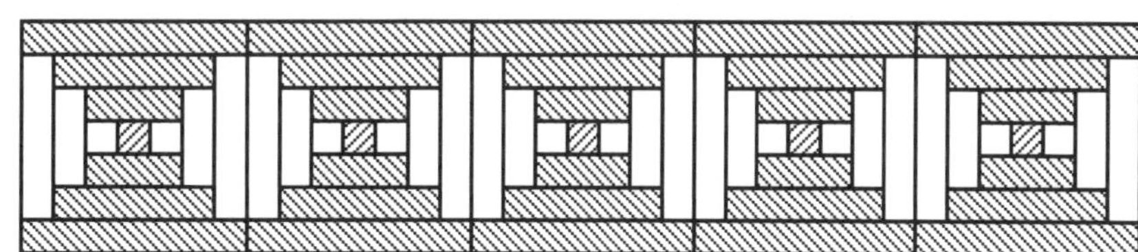

Sew 7 rows together.

Step 10: Finish quilt (see Finishing Chapter)
Piped prairie points
Envelope finish

Quilting suggestions:
Machine stitch in the ditch (in the seam line).
Machine tack
Machine quilt diagonally across the entire quilt.
Top stitch through belt loops or jeans pockets.

Other Court House Step patterns can be found in the book, "Quilt Like A Pro," by Kaye Wood

PROJECT 5: ROCKY ROAD SCRAP QUILT

Left-over pieces from other projects can be turned into quilts that can be used and abused. They are great for picnics, for beach parties, for camping or as a quilt for that extra special pet.

I have many quilts made from left-overs in the classes I teach. The quilt tops were put together--then my students signed their fabric in my quilt.

Strips of many different lengths should be used for variety. However, each row in the quilt has to be made from strips cut the same width. But, each row can be a different width.

Cottons, blends, double knits, corduroy, wool, and denim can all be used. These quilts can be sewn on your sewing machine or serger.

Your scraps can be multi-colored like an old fashioned scrap quilt, or you can plan your color scheme:

monochromatic--e.g. all shades of blue;
primary (red, yellow, green)--great for children;
earthtones, etc.

FINISHED SIZE: Any size

As I work on a strip pieced project, those pieces which are too short to save, I sew together into a long strip, roll the strip up and put a rubber band around it. More pieces are added to the roll with each project. These pieces are then ready to go into another quilted project, and my sewing room is not cluttered with a lot of little pieces which are too small to use.

When your rolled up strip is large enough--it's time to make a scrap quilt.

Step 1: Measure the length needed; then cut pieces that length from the roll. Sew the long strips together until the quilt is wide enough. There's no need to try to match seamlines.

Step 2: Finish your quilt with Piped Prairie Points and an envelope style finish. (See Finishing Chapter).

Quilting suggestions:
For denim quilts, place jean pockets and belt loops at various places on the quilt; top stitch.

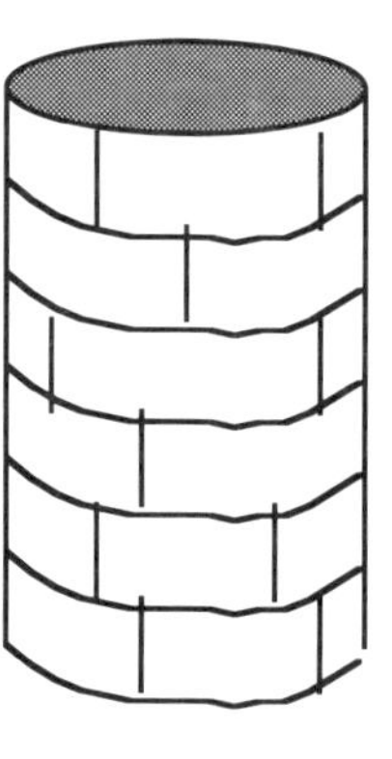

WASTE BASKET COVER

I used denim strips, with a red print at the top and bottom. Measure the circumference of the wastebasket. Cut the strips 2" longer than the circumference. Sew strips together lengthwise into a combination strip. Sew (zigzag) elastic to right side of the top and bottom strips. Turn elastic to wrong side. Stitch (zigzag) along other side of elastic, through the denim. Sew gripper strips (velcro) to the short ends of strips.

PROJECT 6: DECORATE A SHIRT WITH LOG CABIN STRIPS

(7 Log Cabin blocks combined into a decorative trim)

The blocks are sewn together into a strip; then a binding strip is sewn to the block strip. This binding gives a really finished look to the patchwork blocks and the shiny metallic lame fabric helps to really dress it up. However, if you prefer, use a binding cut from a contrasting cotton fabric.

The center (C) in these blocks have strips added to just two sides, and the center square in each block is wider than the strips.

Finished size of each block - 4" x 4"

Fabric needed for 7 blocks:

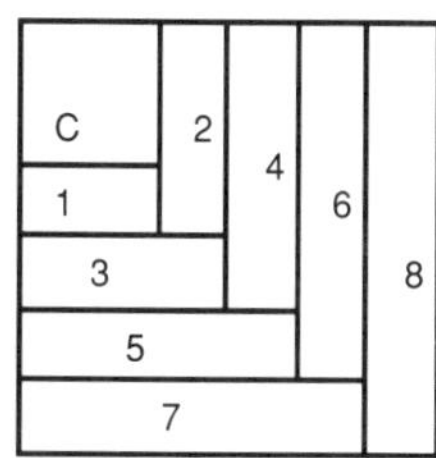

Center (C)	1 strip	3" x 22"
Strip (#1 & 2)	2 strips	1"x 44/45"
Strip (#3 & 4)	2 strips	1"x 44/45"
Strip (#5 & 6)	2 strips	1"x 44/45"
Strip (#7 & 8)	2 strips	1"x 44/45"
binding -	2 strips	1" x 44/45"

(The binding strip makes a decorative edging to the patchwork.)

Follow the Basic Instructions for Log Cabin quilts, Steps 1 & 2

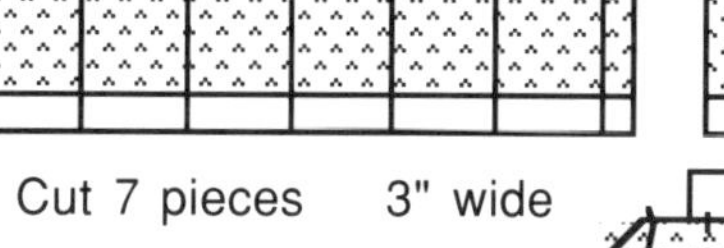

Step 3: Sew these pieces (blocks) to a #2 strip.
Lay the pieces one right after the other on the strip, right sides together.
The center (C) square is away from you as you sew.
The #1 piece is toward you.
The seam allowance will lay toward you.
Press the seam allowances away from the center strip.

Step 4: Cut the #2 strip between where the pieces (blocks) butt together

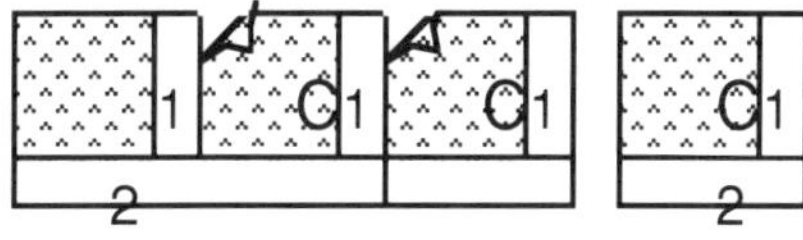

(CUT THE BUTT).

CAUTION: Be sure to only cut the #2 strip, and not the blocks.

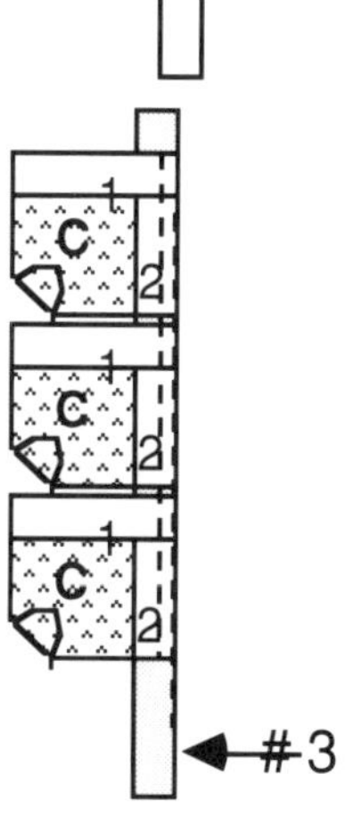

Step 5: Sew these pieces (blocks) to a #3 strip.
Lay the pieces on the strip, right sides together.
The pieces should butt together, but not overlap.
The #2 piece is away from you. The #1 piece lays along the #3 strip.
The C piece is toward you.
The seam allowance lays toward the machine.

Press the seam allowances away from the Center and toward the #3 strip.

Step 6: Cut the #3 strip in between the pieces (blocks).
Use the short vertical lines on the ruler to line up with the seam line.
The edge of the ruler should line up with the cut edge of the block.

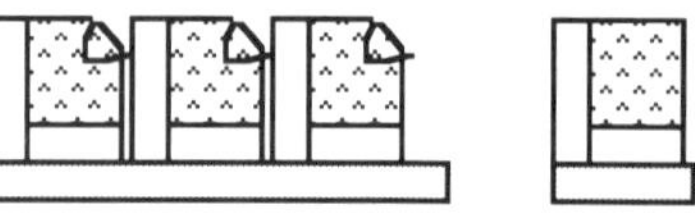

Step 7: Sew these blocks to the #4 strip.
#3 piece will lay toward you; #2 piece will lay along the #4 strip.
Press seam allowances.

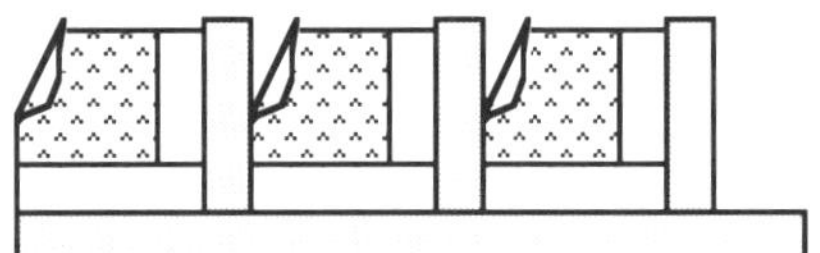

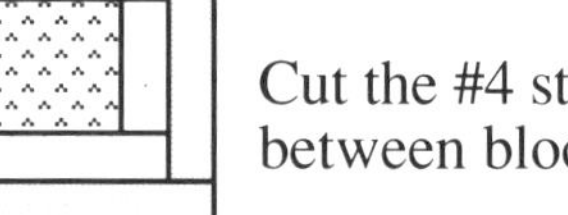

Cut the #4 strip in between blocks.

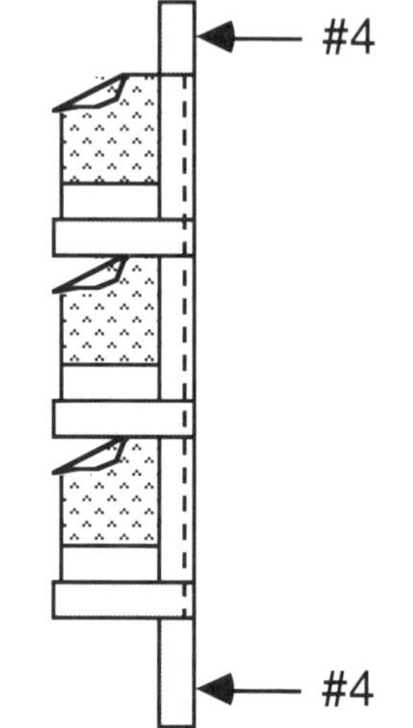

Step 8: Continue adding even strips (#2,4,6,8) to one side of the center.
Add odd strips (#1,3,5,7) to a second side.

Step 9: Sew A, B & C completed blocks together into a strip.
Sew D, E & F blocks together into a strip.

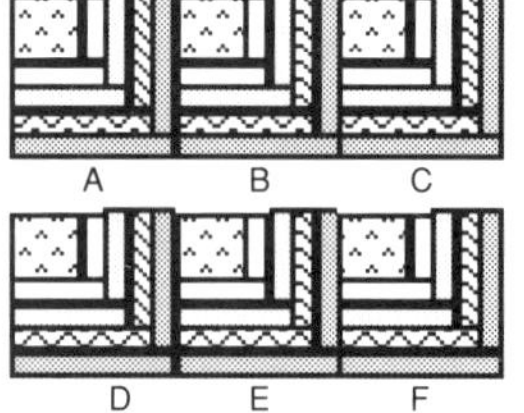

Step 10: Sew a binding strip, right sides together, to the top of both of these block strips.

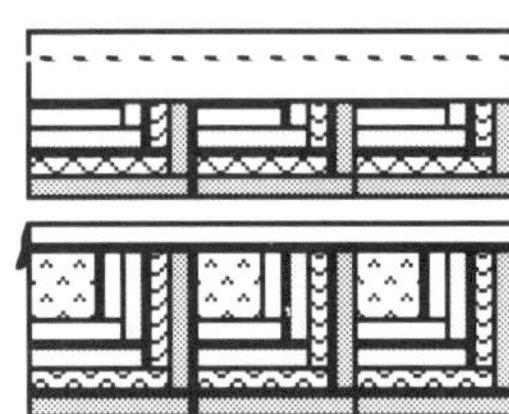

Trim binding strip even with ends of the block strip.
Fold binding strip to wrong side of block strips and pin.
Stitch in ditch between blocks and binding.

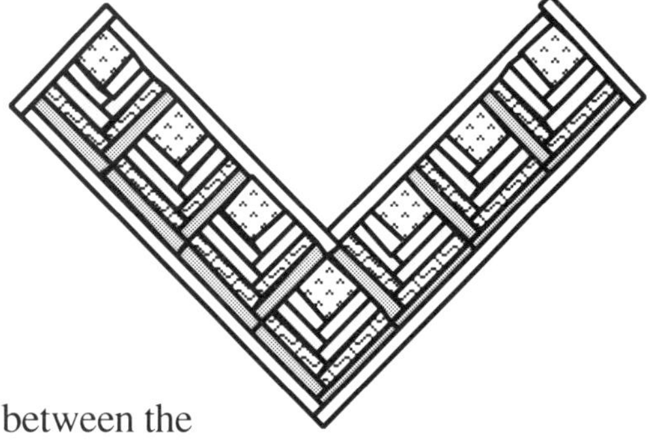

Sew a block between both block strips.
Sew binding strip to the bottom of the block strips; fold to wrong side; stitch in ditch.

Step 11: Place V-shape blocks on shirt. Pin in place.

Attach to shirt by stitching in ditch through seam line between the binding strip and the block strip.

Your patchwork shirt is now ready to wear with pride.

Kaye Wood has more patchwork clothing ideas in her books "Quilt Like A Pro" and "Turn Me Over--I'm Reversible."

Project #1
Log Cabin Placemat

Project #3
Thunderbird Wallhanging

Project #4
Court House Steps Quilt

Project #6
Log Cabin Shirt

Project #7
Chevron Striped Baby Quilt

Project #8
Shining Christmas Star

Project #8
Shining Christmas Star — 3 Sizes

Project #10
Sawtooth Table Runner

Project #9
Jane Ehinger
models her dress

Piped Prairie
Points
finish your
quilt nicely

Project #9
Hot Air Balloons

Project #9
Jane's dress with
Flying Geese in Hot Air Balloons

Kate Larson gets Kaye ready for the next program.

The camera crew ready to go.

Lights! Camera! Action!

Dave Larson directing Kaye and Jane Ehinger.

Ready, Set, Go!

PROJECT 7: CHEVRON STRIPED BABY QUILT

Finished size: 50"x 60"

This is another scrap quilt. If you don't have any scraps, you can always buy fabric especially for a scrap-look quilt.

Each of the 16 blocks in this quilt starts with a 9 1/2" square of fleece. Half of each square is cut from a piece of fabric; the other half is strip pieced in the quilt-as-you-go technique. After all of the blocks and sashing strips are quilted to the fleece and sewn together, the entire quilt is layered on a lightweight batting and backing and machine tied.

If you prefer to quilt-as-you-go on Thermore instead of fleece, you need to add a backing fabric to each block. This backing fabric will not show after the quilt is put together, so any light colored fabric will work.

This quilt can be really feminine looking--
just choose a small floral print for half of the square, pastels for your strips and finish with eyelet trim.
Or, it can be for that special boy in your life--
choose a large print with cowboys or fire engines for the half square and bold coordinating colors for the strips; finish with a binding or large piped prairie points.

Fabric needed:

Half of each square	2/3 yd.
Strips-- scraps cut in various widths-	approximately 1-1/2 yds. total
Sashing strips	1-1/4 yds.
Border #1	1/3 yd.
Border #2	1/3 yd.
fleece or Thermore	enough for a 50"X 60" quilt (it doesn't need to be in one piece)
batting	55" x 65"(lightweight)
backing	55" x 65"
eyelet (optional) -	7 yds.
or binding -	six strips 2-1/2" x 44/45"

Step 1: Cut fleece or Thermore into 16 9-1/2" squares.
(if you use Thermore, also cut 16 9-1/2" squares of fabric for backing)

Step 2: Cut two 10" strips from the fabric for the half-squares.
Cut these strips into 8 10" squares.
Cut each of these 10" squares diagonally into 16 half-squares.

Step 3: Pin the half-squares to the fleece squares.
Baste zigzag (long wide stitch) the outside edges together.

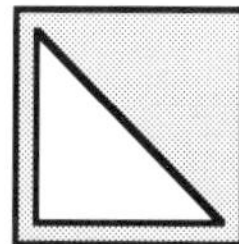

Step 4: Use strips of different widths, all cut on the straight of grain of the fabric (no bias strips).

Lay a strip right sides together on the diagonal cut edge of the half-square.
Sew through all layers.
Open the strip to right side; pin in place;
Trim ends of strip even with fleece.

Continue adding and trimming strips until the square is finished.

Step 5: Square up the squares.
The Starmaker 8 or any two rulers, at right angles, can be used to square up the finished squares.

Baste zigzag (wide, long stitch) all four sides of the squares.

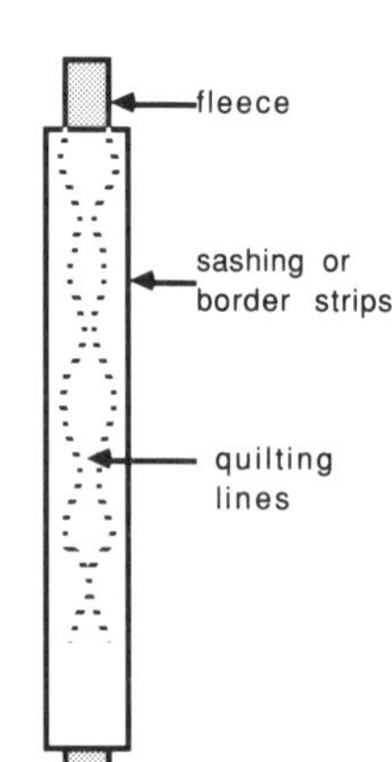

Step 7: Cut 10 sashing strips 3" x 44/45"
Cut 10 fleece or Thermore strips 2" x 44/45"

Center the fleece or Thermore strips under the sashing strips;
Machine quilt the two together;

I used a poly-cotton moire fabric and followed the design with my quilting stitches.
Or try using the decorative machine stitches to quilt.

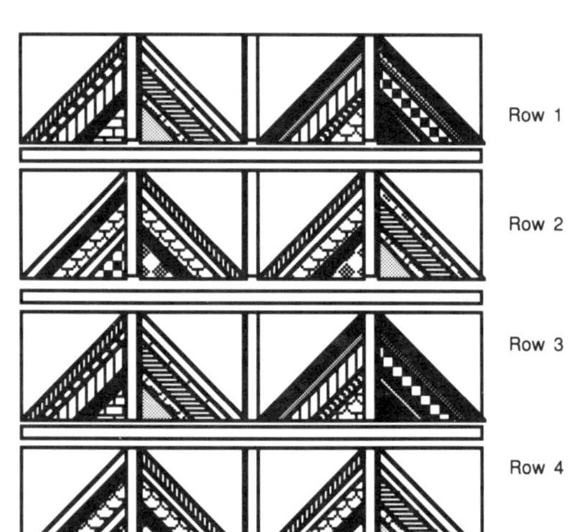

Step 8: Sew blocks and sashing strips into rows.
Trim sashing strips even with blocks.
The fleece or Thermore should just butt together on the back.
If necessary, trim extra fleece so it lays flat.

Sew rows together with sashing strips.
Trim sashing strips even with rows.

Step 9: Quilted borders are added to all four sides of the quilt.

Two extra border strips can be added to the top and bottom of the quilt, if desired. These can be quilted like the sashing strips, or left unquilted for a different effect.

Finish your quilt (see the Finishing Chapter).
Layer the quilt
Machine tie with bows for girls, colored string for boys.
Bind edges or finish with eyelet.

PROJECT 8: SHINING CHRISTMAS STAR

(Three sizes: 6" - 8" - 16")

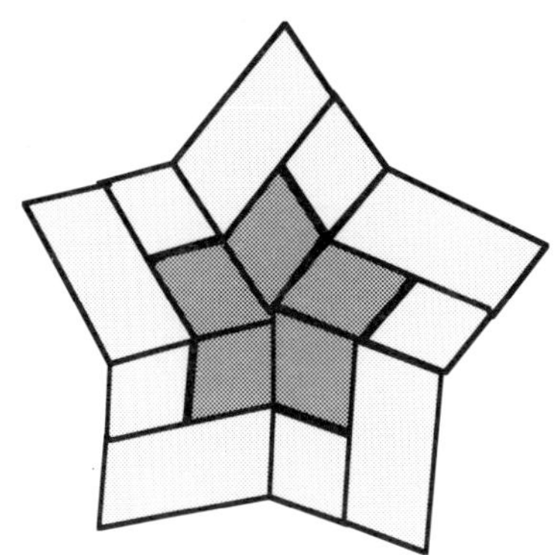

Three different size stars are shown--all made exactly the same. The small and medium sized stars may be stuffed for Christmas tree ornaments; the large star can takes its place on the top of your tree. Or, they may be lined and quilted and used under candleholders for a Christmas centerpiece.

The center of each block is made from silver lame. One strip of turquoise lame is added to only two sides of the center. If you prefer, make your stars out of Christmas prints.

These stars all have 5 points. To make it easier to piece these stars, we want to make sure all the angles are accurate--therefore we will strip piece these stars and use the Starmaker 5 tool.

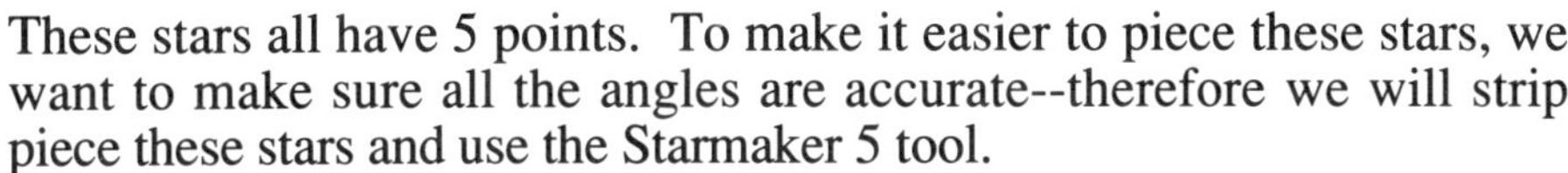
THIS IS A NEW AND BETTER WAY TO PIECE TOGETHER 5-POINTED STARS.
TRY THESE PIECING IDEAS ON ALL THE 5-POINTED STARS IN MY OTHER BOOKS.

Fabric needed:

	Small star-6"	Medium star-8"	Large star-16"
center (C)	1-1/2"x 10"	2" x 15"	3" x 20"
#1 & #2	1-1/2" x 44/45"	2" x 44/45"	two 3" x 44/45"
backing	7" x 7"	9" x 9"	16" x 16"

Poly-down fiberfill
Silver cord or thread 6" for each ornament

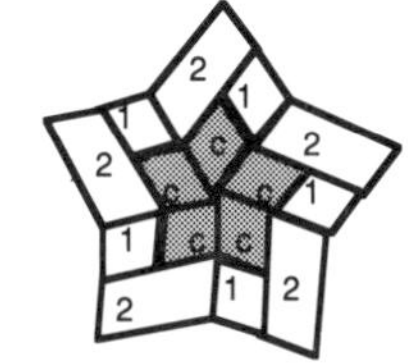

Step 1: Follow the basic instructions for Log Cabin quilts, Step 1.
Press using low heat--lame can melt and mess up your iron.

Step 2: Cut the far right of the combination strip.
Use the Starmaker 5 by lining up the bottom of the Starmaker 5 with the bottom of the strip.
Cut.

Step 3: Measure the slanted side of the C (silver lame) strip, including the seam allowance.

This is the only time you will need to measure.

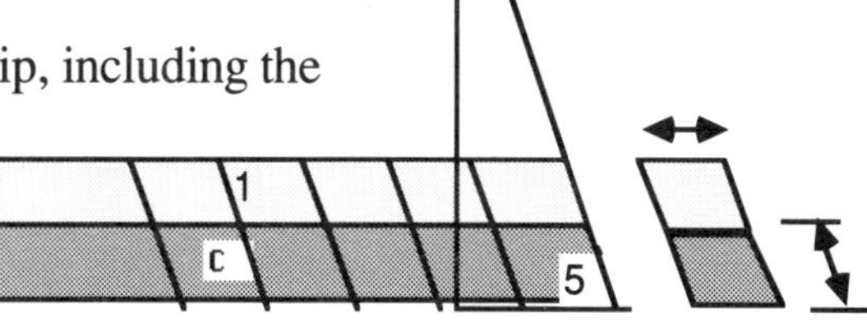

This measurement should then be marked along the top of the combination strip.

Cut 5 pieces from the combination strip (one for each point of the star) .

Line up the bottom of the Starmaker 5 with the bottom of the strip, and the slanted side of the Starmaker 5 with the marks you made along the top of the strip.

Step 4: Sew these 5 pieces (blocks) to a #2 strip.
Lay the pieces one right after the other on the strip, right sides together.
The center (C) diamond is toward you as you sew;
the #1 piece is toward the machine or away from you.

Your pieces should line up perfectly on the strip.
If the pieces are wider or narrower than the #2 strip,
you need to go back to Step 3 and recut them.

Step 5: Use the Starmaker 5 to cut the #2 strip accurately.
Line up the bottom of the Starmaker 5 with the bottom of the strip, and the slanted side of the Starmaker 5 with the cut edge of the pieces (blocks).

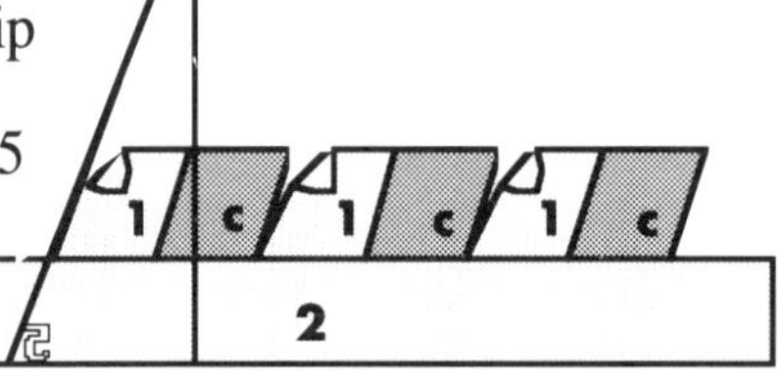

Step 6: Sew the points of the star together.
Sew two points together, start sewing at the very tip of the center.
Match seam lines by finger pinning or use a pin.
Sew to the very end of the two pieces.
Sew another two points together the same way.

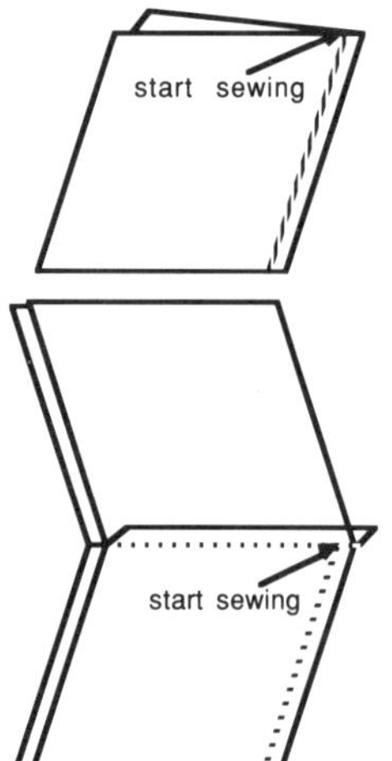

Step 7: Sew these two sets of points together,
BUT, start sewing at the seamline between the points by putting the needle down through the seamline;
lock your stitches by dropping the feed dogs (or put stitch length on 0) and stitch 3 or 4 stitches in place.
Raise the feed dogs and sew to the end.

(In Step 9, I'll tell you how to turn your star even though you've sewn to the end here).

Step 8: Sew the remaining point by matching the center points, put needle down through seam line, lock your stitches. Sew to the end of the piece.
Sew the other side of the point, starting at center seamline, and sew to the end.

Step 9: Cut a backing piece the same size as your star.
Lay the cord for hanging on the right side of one of the points of the star, cut ends toward the outside of the star.

Sew right sides together, leaving an opening for turning and stuffing.
NOW, remove the stitches from the outside of each point back to the seamline around the outside edges.

This will prevent the little hole you sometimes get at the inside angle when you stop your stitching at the seam line.

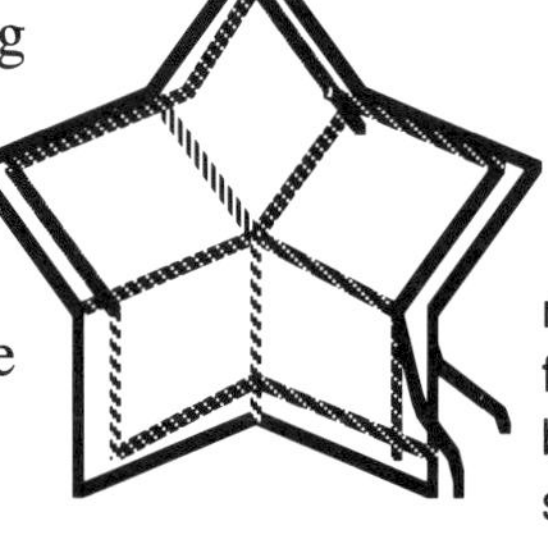

remove stitches from outside edge back to the stitching line

Step 10: Turn right sides out. Stuff your star if it is an ornament, and hand stitch the opening.
Or, if it is a table decoration, stitch the opening, and quilt the star.

Other 5-pointed stars can be found in these books by Kaye Wood:
"Quilt Like A Pro", "Serger Patchwork Projects", "Strip Quilting Projects" and her video "Starmaker Quilt Designs.

PROJECT 9: HOT AIR BALLOONS
made from Log Cabin Triangles

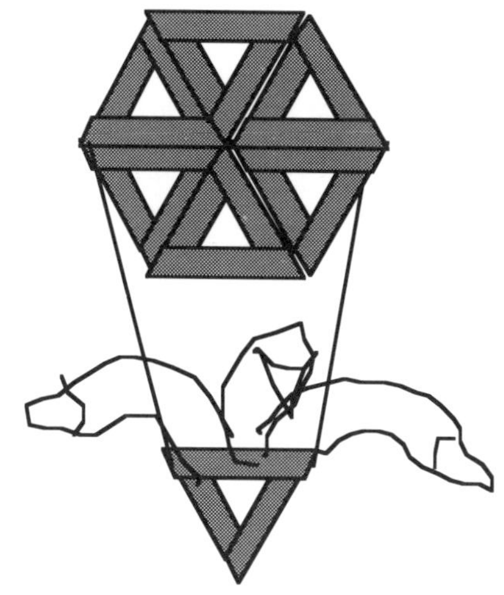

Geese fly south for the winter. And Jane Ehinger created an easy way for these lazy, or smart, geese to fly--in hot air balloons.

The balloons are strip-pieced Log Cabin triangles in bright crayon colors.

The baskets that hold our geese are black strip-pieced Log Cabin triangles.

Directions for the geese are included. Together they are appliqued and make a fun decoration.

Fabric for each pieced triangle block:

centers-white	2" x 2-1/2"
strips	1-1/2" x 15"

Step 1: Use the Starmaker 6 to cut triangles from the white strip. Cut one white triangle for each block.

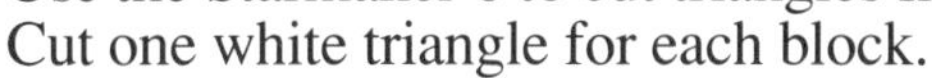

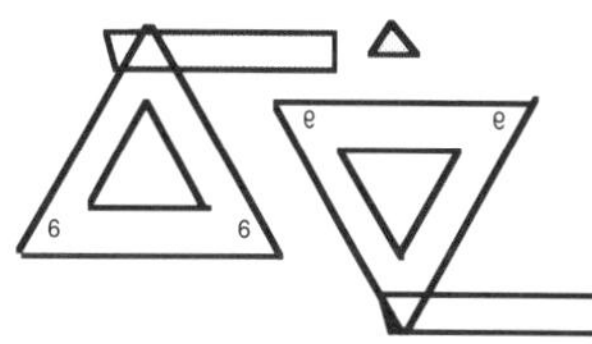

Step 2: Cut strips 1-1/2" wide

Sew a strip to one side of center triangles.
Sew with strip on top, triangle underneath.

Sewing with the triangle underneath will eliminate stretching the slightly bias edges of the center triangle.
Chain stitch, if making more than 1 triangle, but leave 2" between triangles.

Press seam allowances toward the strip; away from center triangle.

Step 3: Cut both ends of the #1 strip by placing the point of the Starmaker 6 at the point of the triangle opposite the new strip.

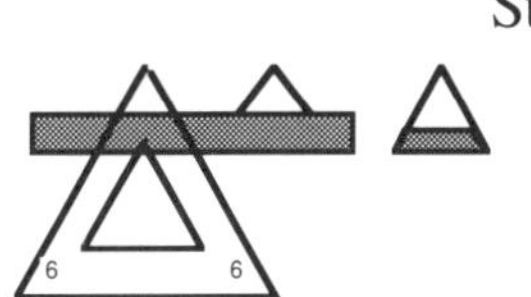

Step 4: Sew #2 strip to second side of center triangle.
Sew with strip on top, triangle underneath.
Chain stitch but leave 2" between triangles.
Press seam allowances toward the strip.
Use the Starmaker 6 to cut both ends of the #2 strip.

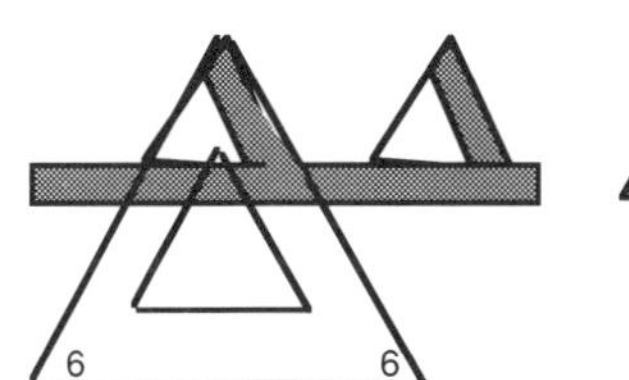

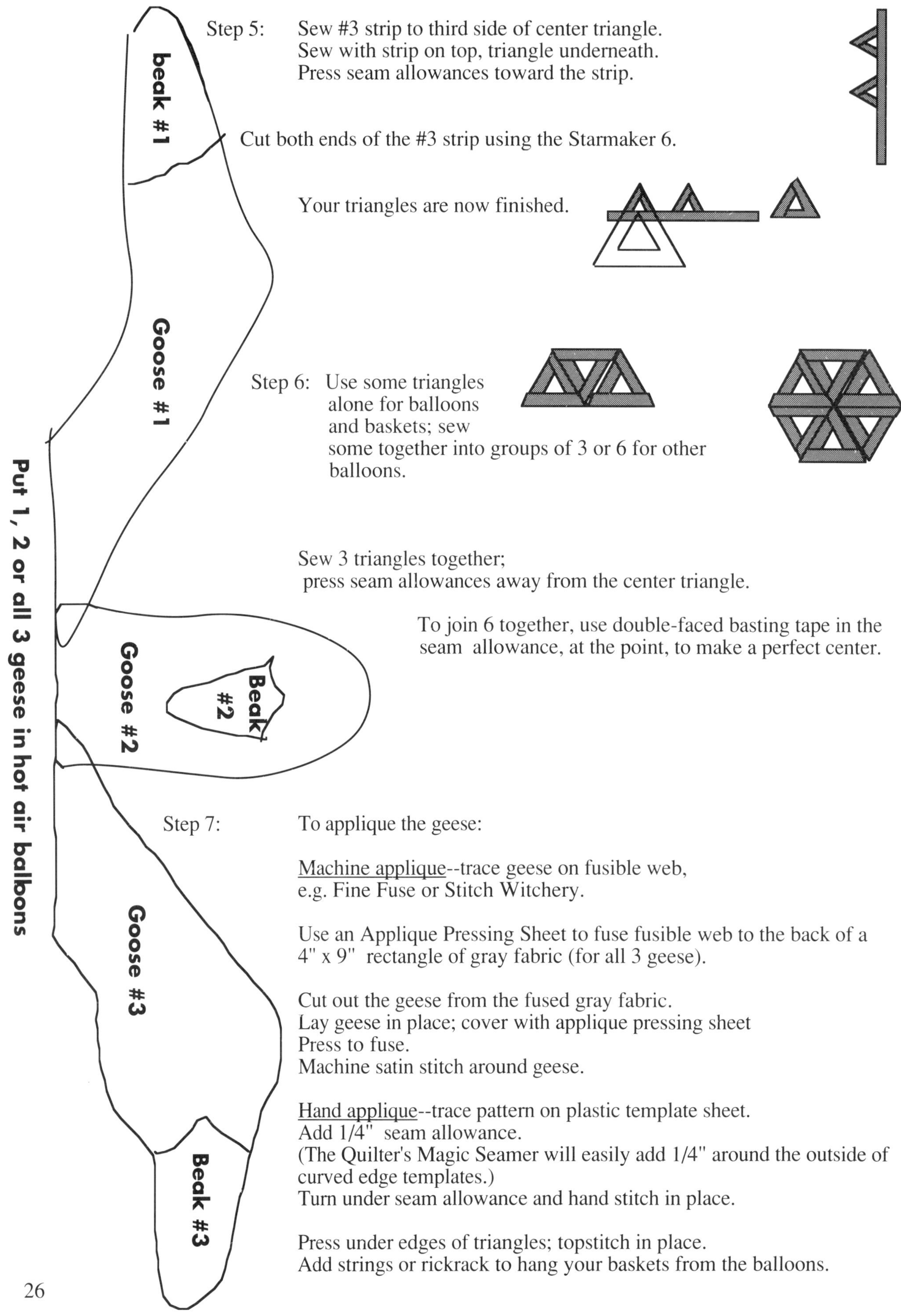

Step 5: Sew #3 strip to third side of center triangle.
Sew with strip on top, triangle underneath.
Press seam allowances toward the strip.

Cut both ends of the #3 strip using the Starmaker 6.

Your triangles are now finished.

Step 6: Use some triangles alone for balloons and baskets; sew some together into groups of 3 or 6 for other balloons.

Sew 3 triangles together;
press seam allowances away from the center triangle.

To join 6 together, use double-faced basting tape in the seam allowance, at the point, to make a perfect center.

Step 7: To applique the geese:

Machine applique--trace geese on fusible web, e.g. Fine Fuse or Stitch Witchery.

Use an Applique Pressing Sheet to fuse fusible web to the back of a 4" x 9" rectangle of gray fabric (for all 3 geese).

Cut out the geese from the fused gray fabric.
Lay geese in place; cover with applique pressing sheet
Press to fuse.
Machine satin stitch around geese.

Hand applique--trace pattern on plastic template sheet.
Add 1/4" seam allowance.
(The Quilter's Magic Seamer will easily add 1/4" around the outside of curved edge templates.)
Turn under seam allowance and hand stitch in place.

Press under edges of triangles; topstitch in place.
Add strings or rickrack to hang your baskets from the balloons.

PROJECT 10: SAWTOOTH TABLE RUNNER with Log Cabin Triangles

Finished size: 19" x 80"

This table runner will brighten up any meal.

It is made from strip-pieced Log Cabin triangles combined with solid triangles. The bottom of each triangle is a light (or accent) color. The other two sides are darker; two of them form a diamond shape across your table.

The Starmaker 8 quilting tool is used to strip piece these triangles--it eliminates the need for templates and insures that the angles will be accurate.

The traditional method of piecing would require you to make 7 different templates to make these triangles, and then the angles could still be a problem.

When sewing triangles, it is best to sew the center triangle and strips together with the triangle on the bottom and the strips on top--because all sides of the triangle cannot be cut on the grainline of the fabric and there is a chance the off-grain sides could stretch if sewn with the triangles on top.

20 pieced triangles and 18 plain triangles are used in this project.

Fabric needed:

center triangles	1 strip	5" x 44/45"
#1 light	3 strips	1-1/2" x 44/45"
#2 dark	4 strips	1-1/2" x 44/45"
#3 dark	5 strips	1-1/2" x 44/45"
#4 light	4 strips	1-1/2" x 44/45"
#5 dark	6 strips	1-1/2" x 44/45"
#6 dark	6 strips	1-1/2" x 44/45"
solid colored triangles & binding		1 yd
binding alone	5 strips	3" x 44/45"
backing fabric		20" x 85"
batting, fleece or Thermore		20" x 85"

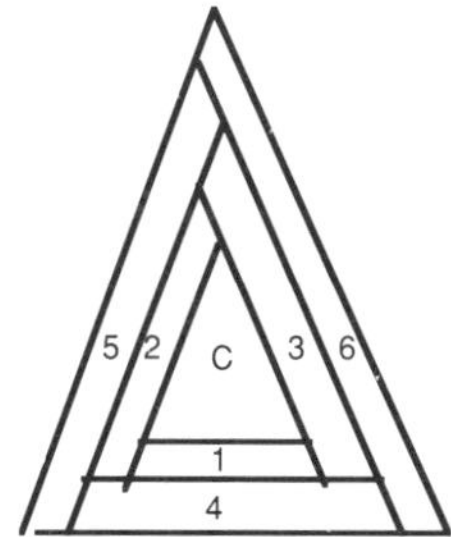

Step 1: Cut the center triangle strip using the Starmaker 8 by placing the point of the Starmaker 8 at the top of the strip.

The wedge lines on the Starmaker 8 are parallel to the bottom of the strip and will help keep your triangles even. Cut the triangle on both sides of the Starmaker 8.

Cut the second triangle with the Starmaker 8 upside down. The point will now be at the bottom of the strip.

Continue cutting until you have 20 triangles.

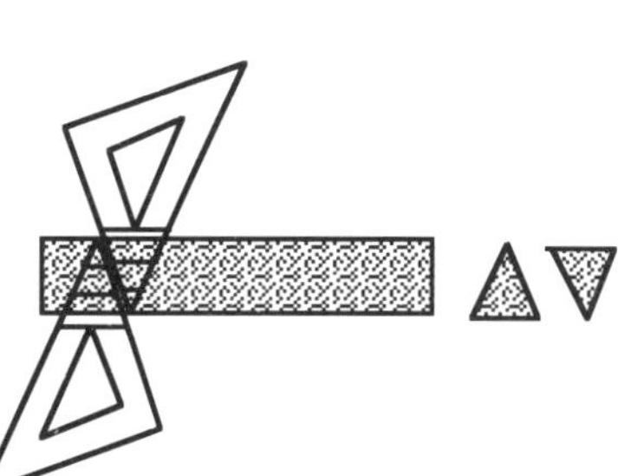

Step 2: Sew #1 strip, right sides together, to the short side of all 20 triangles. Sew with the triangles underneath, the strip on top.

Chain stitch one triangle after the other, but leave 1 inch between each of the triangles.

Press seam allowances away from center triangle.
(See pressing instructions)

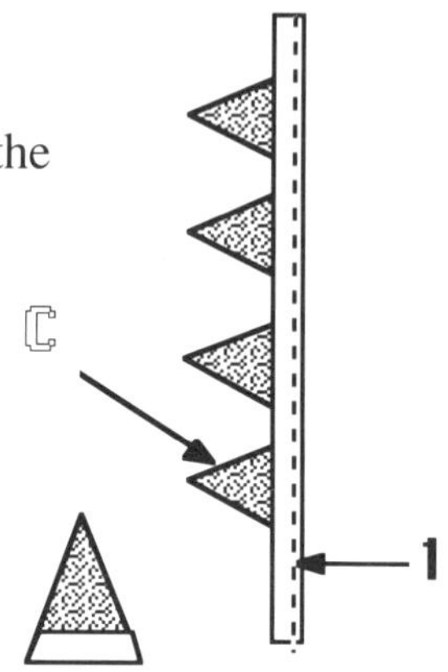

Step 3: Place the point of the Starmaker 8 on the top of the triangle.

Cut both sides of the strip.

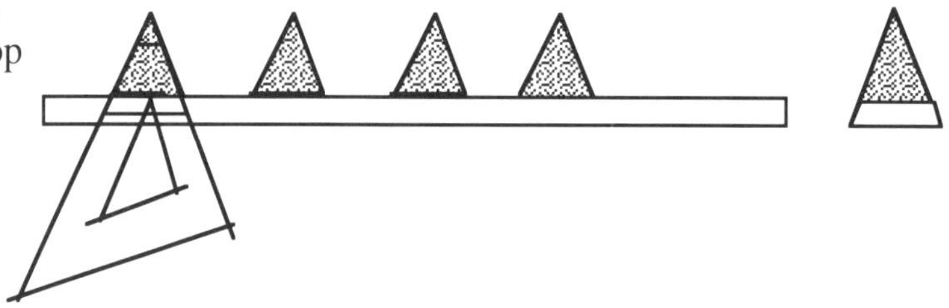

Step 4: Sew #2 strip, right sides together, to the left side of the triangles.
Chain stitch one triangle after the other, but leave 2-1/2" between each of the triangles.

Press seam allowances away from center triangle.

Step 5: To cut the ends of the strips into the triangle shape, two different types of cuts are necessary:

On the bottom of the triangle, place the center opening and line on the
Starmaker 8 on the seam line of the #2 strip, as shown;
the edge of
the Starmaker lays along the edge of the #1 strip.

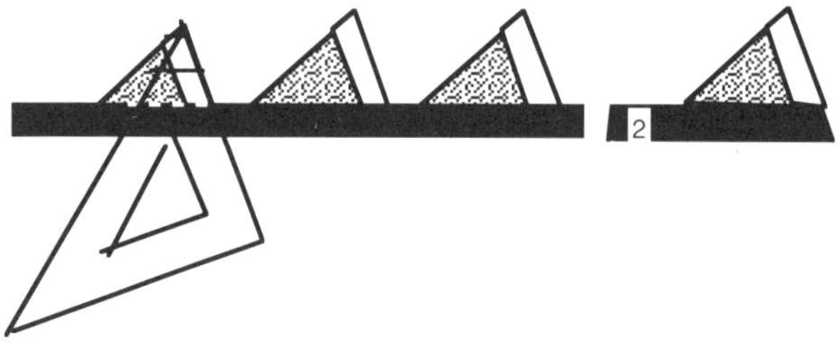

To cut the other end of the strip, line up the Starmaker 8 with the edge of the #2 strip and the edge of the center triangle.

Step 6: Sew Strip #3 to the right side of the 20 triangles.
Chain stitch one triangle after another but, leave 2-1/2" between each triangle.

Press seam allowances away from the center triangle.

Step 7: To cut the ends of the strips into the triangle shape, two different types of cuts are necessary:

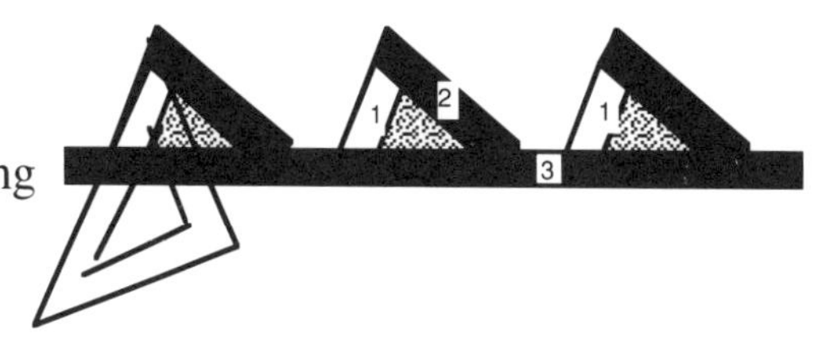

On the bottom of the triangle, place the center opening and line on the Starmaker 8 on the seam line of the #3 strip;
the edge of the Starmaker lays along the edge of the #1 strip.

To cut the other end of the strip, line up the Starmaker 8 with the edge of the #3 strip and the edge of #2 strip.

Step 8: Continue adding strips #4, 5 and 6 following Steps 2 thru 6.

Step 9: To cut the plain triangles, measure the height of the pieced triangles (approximately 11"). Cut 2 strips of fabric that width (approx.11") x 44/45".
Use the wedge lines on the Starmaker 8, just like Step 1, to cut these strips into 18 triangles.

Step 10: Sew 10 pieced triangles and 9 solid triangles into rows.

Press seam allowances away from each point for easier matching.

Step 11: Sew rows together. Use double-faced basting tape to match points exactly (see Matching Seamlines in the Introduction).

Step 12: Cut backing & batting (Thermore or fleece) the same shape as completed top.

Finish your table runner (see Finishing Chapter).
Layer it, quilt it, and add a binding.

Kaye Wood has more designs using the Starmaker 8 in these books:
"Quilt Like A Pro," " Turn Me Over--I'm Reversible,"
"Serger Patchwork Projects," " Strip Quilting Projects,"
and on her video: "Starmaker Quilt Designs."

PROJECT 11: REVERSIBLE BASKET

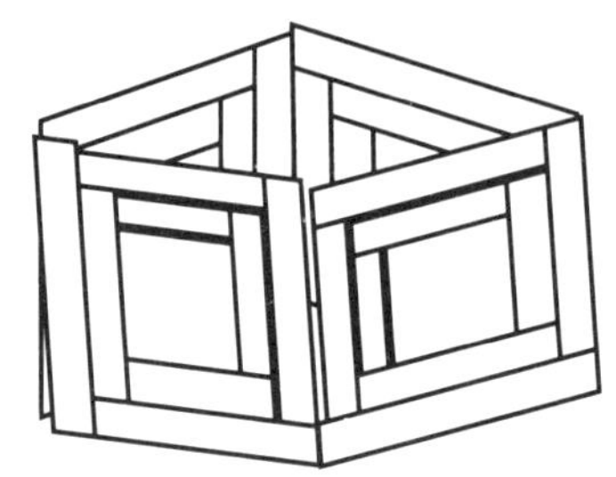

The inside of your basket will look as good as the outside, and can even become the outside with this reversible basket. And your needlework will have a home of its own in this basket on the floor next to your favorite chair.

Five quilt-as-you-go reversible Log Cabin blocks are joined together with an enclosed decorative seam. Make an extra block for a top for your basket.

Finished Size: 12-1/2" high by 12-1/2" wide

This is a perfect project for your serger, but it can also be done on your sewing machine, using both a straight stitch and a basting zigzag (long, wide) stitch. Instructions for both are included. If you only have a straight stitch machine, instead of overcasting the edges, trim the batting from the seam allowances.

The BASIC INSTRUCTIONS FOR LOG CABIN QUILTS will be followed with the following exception:

There are 2 tops to these blocks, instead of a right and wrong side. We'll refer to them as Side A and Side B.

Each time a strip is added, it is added on both Side A and Side B. A strip of quilt batting is also added all in one step.

Fabric needed:

	Side A	Side B
Center	4" x 22" strip	4" x 22" strip
#1 & 2	2 strips 3" x 44/45"	2 strips 3" x 44/4
#3 & 4	2 strips 3" x 44/45"	2 strips 3" x 44/45"
#5 & 6	3 strips 3" x 44/45"	3 strips 3" x 44/45"
#7 & 8	4 strips 3" x 44/45"	4 strips 3" x 44/45"
Batting	Crib size package of HiLoft	
Binding	3 strips 1-3/4" x 44/45"	

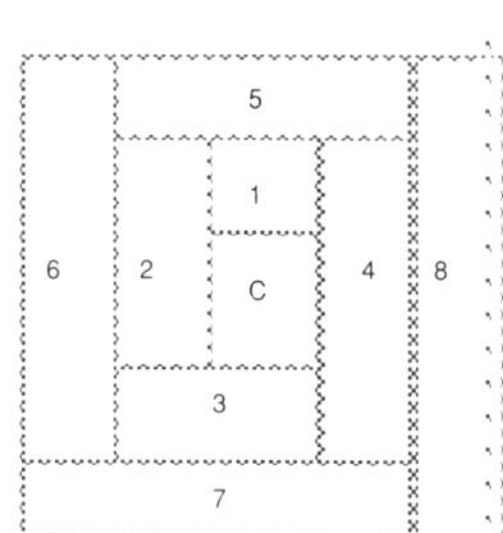

Step 1: Cut the batting lengthwise into one 4"x22" strip and about ten 3" wide strips (more batting strips can be cut as needed).

Step 2: Layer the

Center A strip, right side up,
4" strip of Batting
Center B strip, right side down.

Pin carefully.
Overcast both long edges with a basting zigzag stitch (long & wide); or serge.

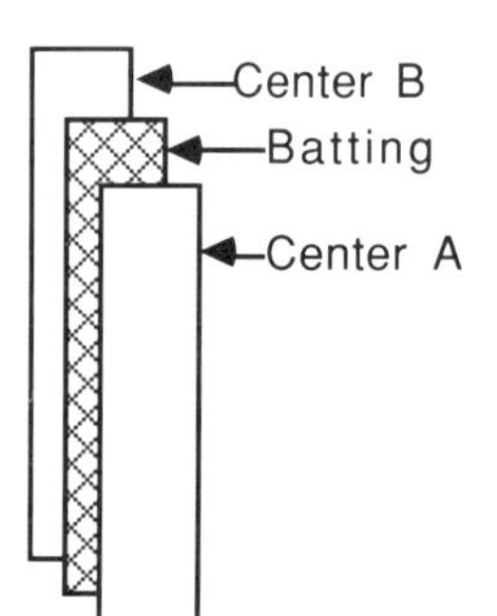

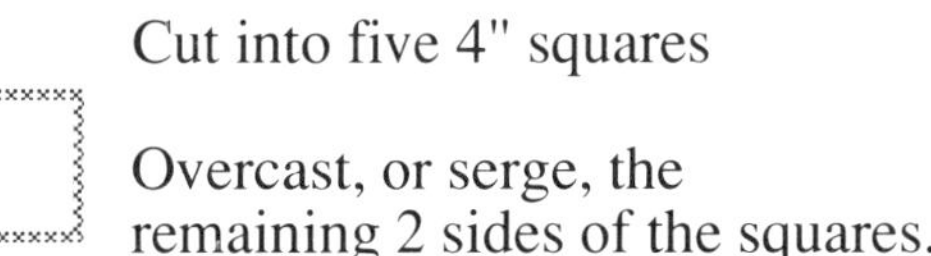

Cut into five 4" squares

Overcast, or serge, the remaining 2 sides of the squares.

If your machine or serger pushes the top layer ahead of the bottom layer, you need to loosen the pressure on the presser foot.

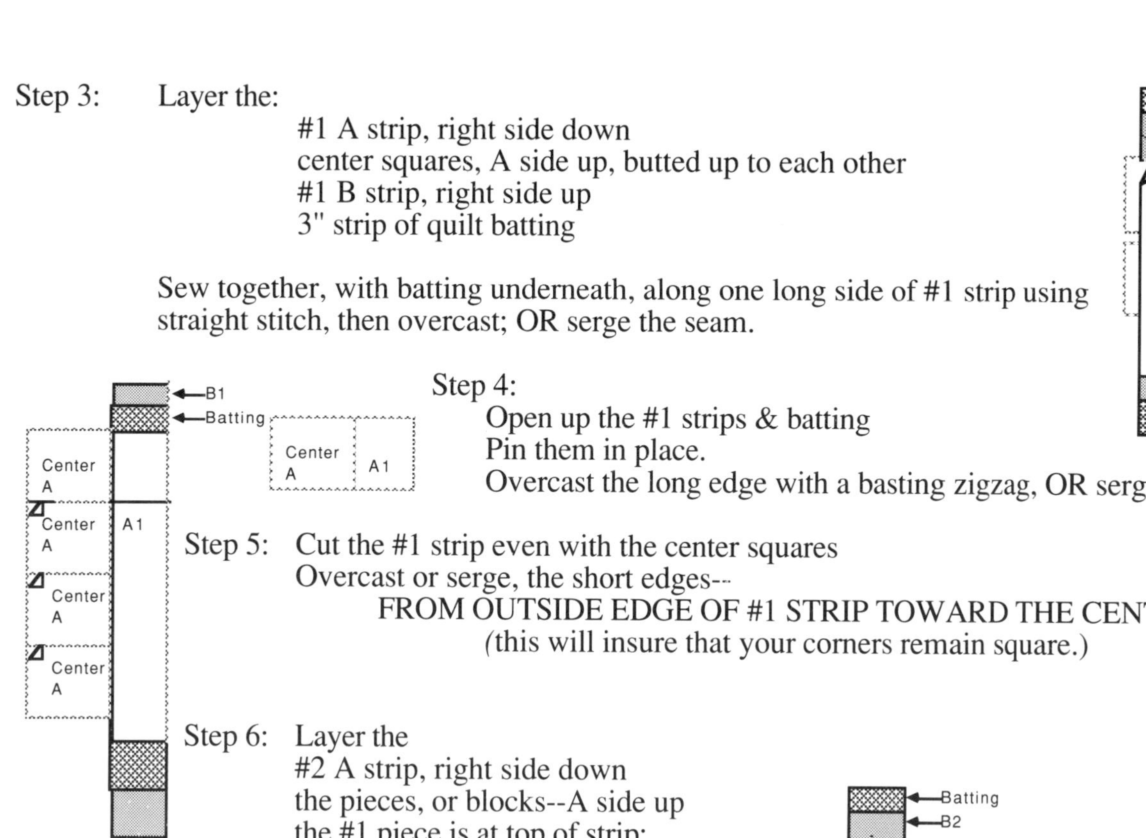

Step 3: Layer the:

#1 A strip, right side down
center squares, A side up, butted up to each other
#1 B strip, right side up
3" strip of quilt batting

Sew together, with batting underneath, along one long side of #1 strip using straight stitch, then overcast; OR serge the seam.

Step 4:

Open up the #1 strips & batting
Pin them in place.
Overcast the long edge with a basting zigzag, OR serge.

Step 5: Cut the #1 strip even with the center squares
Overcast or serge, the short edges--
FROM OUTSIDE EDGE OF #1 STRIP TOWARD THE CENTER--
(this will insure that your corners remain square.)

Step 6: Layer the
#2 A strip, right side down
the pieces, or blocks--A side up
the #1 piece is at top of strip;
the Center piece at bottom
#2 B strip, right side up
3" strip of batting

Sew with straight stitch, then overcast;
OR serge.

Open up the #2 strips and batting
Overcast, or serge, long edge of strip #2

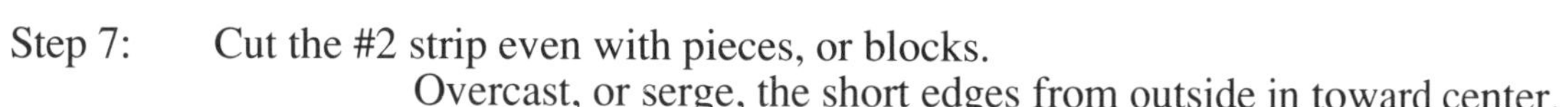

Step 7: Cut the #2 strip even with pieces, or blocks.
Overcast, or serge, the short edges from outside in toward center.

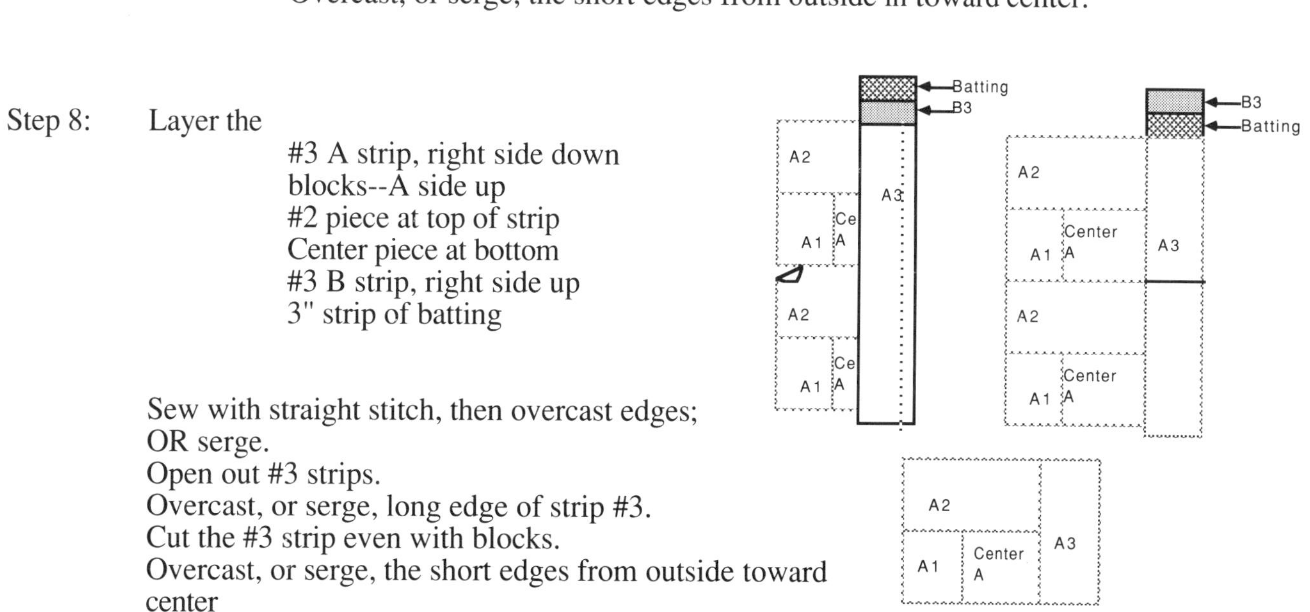

Step 8: Layer the

#3 A strip, right side down
blocks--A side up
#2 piece at top of strip
Center piece at bottom
#3 B strip, right side up
3" strip of batting

Sew with straight stitch, then overcast edges;
OR serge.
Open out #3 strips.
Overcast, or serge, long edge of strip #3.
Cut the #3 strip even with blocks.
Overcast, or serge, the short edges from outside toward center

Step 9: Layer the

#4 A strip, right side down
blocks--A side up
#3 piece at top of strip
#1 piece at bottom of strip
#4 A strip, right side up
3" strip of batting

Sew, then overcast; OR serge.
Open out #4 strips.
Overcast or serge long edge of strip #4.
Cut the #4 strip even with blocks.
Overcast, or serge, the short edges from outside toward center.

Step 10: Continue adding strips, counterclockwise on side A.
The last strip added to side A is always at the top on the new strip, or toward the machine, when sewing.

Step 11: Lay out four completed blocks in the desired design (these 4 will form the sides of the basket.) Join these 4 blocks together with **enclosed seams**:

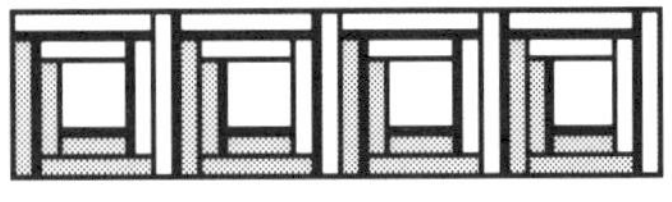

sew 4 blocks together
using enclosed seams

Cut binding strips 1-3/4" wide.
Fold in half lengthwise, see Finishing Chapter.

Pin 2 blocks, sides B, together.
Pin raw edges of binding strip even with edges of blocks.
Sew, or serge, through all layers

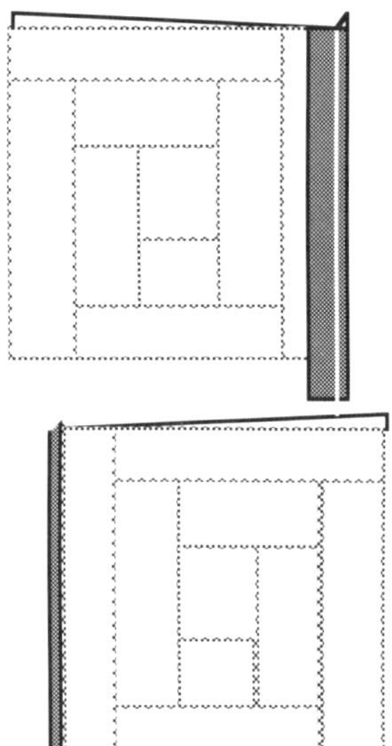

Enclosed seam-- bring binding strip over seam allowances and pin even with raw edge of blocks. The fold should lay on the seamline Topstitch through the fold and seam allowances.

Sew the first and last blocks together into a circle using an enclosed seam.

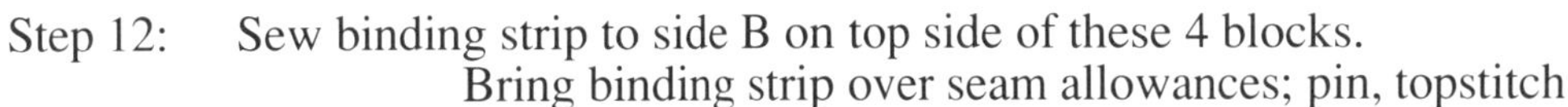

Step 12: Sew binding strip to side B on top side of these 4 blocks.
Bring binding strip over seam allowances; pin, topstitch.

Step 13: Sew bottom block to 4 sides of the basket with enclosed seam.
Sew with the binding strip underneath.
Sew to 1/4" from corner, with needle in fabric, pivot and sew off the corner--just like mitering a corner in Finishing Chapter.

On the next side, start by locking stitches at a 1/4" seam allowance; then sew to the next corner.

Your basket is finished, reversible and quilted--and ready for filling.

For more reversible projects, take a look at these books and video by Kaye Wood:
"Quilt Like A Pro", "Turn Me Over--I'M Reversible,"
"Serger Patchwork Projects" and "Strip Quilting Projects"
and the video: "Reversible Quilts."

PROJECT 12: PINEAPPLE WALL HANGING

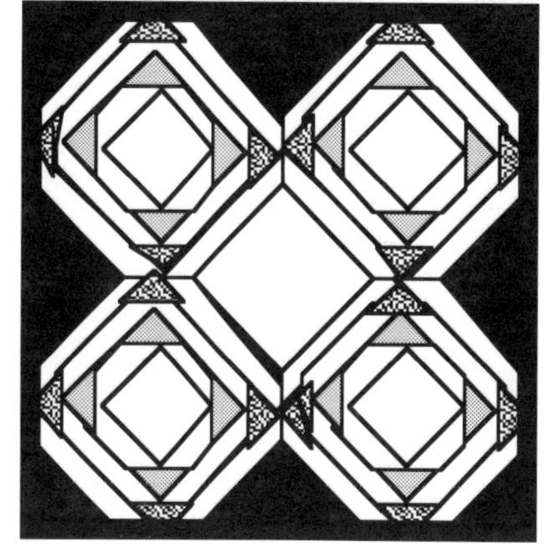

The Pineapple is a more-difficult-looking project, but with the tips and techniques that are included here, it becomes another easy project.

Instead of working with 7 different templates, we will strip piece our Pineapple and use the Starmaker 8 quilting tool for the accurate angles we need.

We will start with a large center floral square, add strips to each side, then add corner strips. Four blocks, sewn together with a joiner block, and set on-point, will make an interesting wall hanging. Machine quilting in the ditch around the strips, and free-motion machine quilting around the central floral design highlight our Pineapple design.

Finished size: 20" x 20"

Fabric Needed:

Centers	five 5" squares centered on large flowers		
#1	lt. mauve	2 strips	1 1/2" x 44/45"
#2	lt. blue	2 strips	1 1/2" x 44/45"
#3	med. mauve	3 strips	1 1/2" x 44/45"
#4	med. blue	2 strips	1 1/2" x 44/45"
#5	dark mauve	3 strips	1 1/2" x 44/45"
#6	black	1 strip	4" x 25"
Backing fabric:		21" x 21"	
Binding		2 strips	1-1/2" x 44/45"
Batting:		21" x 21"	

Step 1: Sew #1 strips to the two sides of all 4 centers.
Cut the strip even with the squares.
Press seam allowances away from the center.

Sew a #1 strip to the top and bottom of all 4 centers.
Press seam allowances away from the center square.

Step 2: Use the Starmaker 8 to cut the strips at an angle--
Line up the guideline (& center opening) on the Starmaker with the seamline between the center square and #1 strip. The slanted edge of the Starmaker should be 1/4" (for seam allowance) away from the corner of the center square.
Cut the #1 strips on this angle on all four corners.

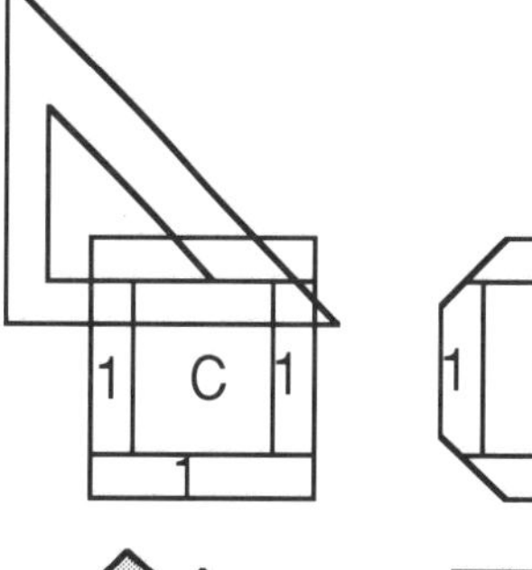

Step 3: Sew #2 strips to the blocks at each corner of the center squares and even with the angled cut of the #1 strips.

Cut the ends of the #2 strips with the Starmaker 8--
Line up the guideline (& center opening) with the seamline of the #2 strip. Cut the ends even with the #1 strip.

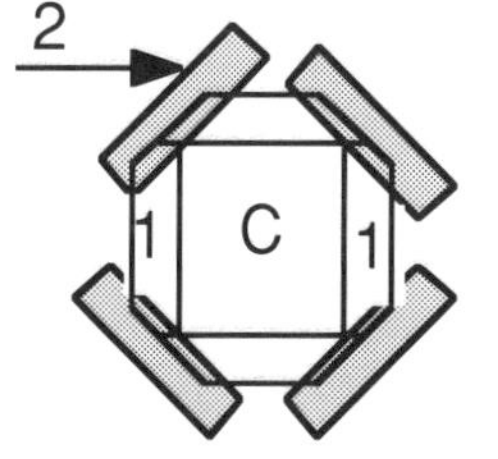

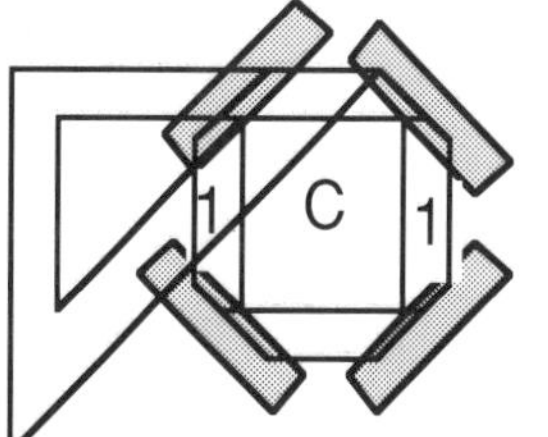

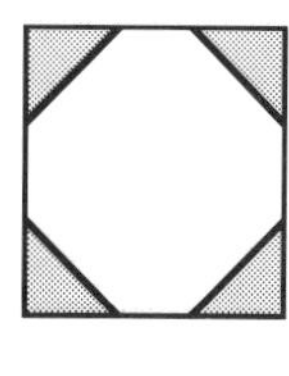

Step 4: Sew #3 strips next to #1 strips on all 4 sides of your block.

Cut the ends of the #3 strips using the Starmaker 8--
Line up the guideline & center opening of the Starmaker 8 with the seamline of strip #3.
Cut the ends even with the #2 strip.

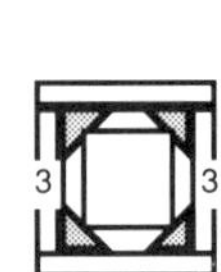

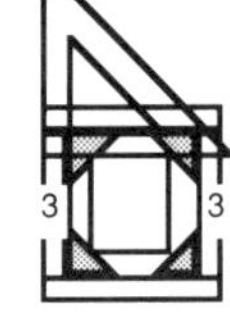

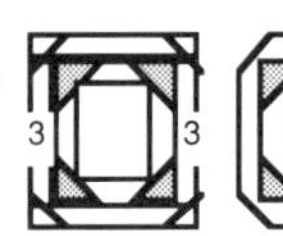

Step 5: Continue adding #4 and #5 strips in the same way.
Strips #1, 3, & 5 are on the sides of the center square.
Strips #2 and 4 are on the corners.

Step 6: Cut six 4" squares from the 4" black strip. Cut these six squares diagonally into 12 triangles.

Sew these triangles to the 3 outside corners of each block.

Cutting triangles in this way will give you a straight grain on the outside edges of your block.
Square up the outside edges of the black triangles, if necessary, using the Starmaker 8.

Step 7: Sew two pieced blocks together on opposite sides of a 5" floral square.
Press seam allowances.

Sew the two remaining pieced blocks to the opposite sides of the 5" square from seam line to seam line.
Sew sides of pieced blocks together from seam line to outside edge.

Step 8: Finish your wallhanging (see the Finishing Chapter).
Layer your quilt carefully.
Machine quilt in the ditch around the outside of the square that forms in the center (where the 4 blocks join together).

To do Free-motion quilting around the flowers in the center and in the center of each block--
- lower the feed dogs (or set stitch length at 0)
- remove the presser foot from your machine
- set machine for straight stitch; loosen upper thread tension
- place quilt in an embroidery hoop; bring bobbin thread up through fabric and hold both threads.
- lower presser foot bar (so there will be tension on thread)
- stitch around flowers without turning hoop--just move it side to side, back & forth

Add a binding.
Hang your quilt with hang tabs or by adding a sleeve to the back.

More Starmaker 8 quilting designs by Kaye Wood are in:
"Quilt Like A Pro," " Turn Me Over--I'm Reversible,"
"Serger Patchwork Projects," " Strip Quilting Projects,"
and the video: "Starmaker Quilt Designs."

CHAPTER 3:

HOW TO FINISH A QUILT

Now that your quilt top is finished, you have to choose how to finish it and what kind of batting or filler to use. The choice of finishes depends on--

How your quilt will be used - will it be used for a baby and therefore washed a lot. Or will it be a family heirloom or on display to be judged at a quilt show.
How it will be displayed - with hang tabs or a sleeve or will it be used on a bed.
Who it was made for - an eyelet finish is nice for a feminine touch, but a binding might be better for a boy.

TYPES OF BATTING and FILLINGS

There are several different types of fillers for your quilted items depending on the look you want and how your quilted item will be used.

Fleece--is good for placemats and tablecloths
Thermore by Hobbs-- especially good for quilted clothing because it drapes so well; also good for placemats, tablecloths and anywhere that you want a light weight batting with drapability.
Bonded Batting, such as Hobbs' Polydown batting--used for most quilts and quilted projects
HiLoft Bonded Batting, such as Hobbs' Cloud Loft batting--especially good for comforter weight quilts and reversible quilts.
Fiberfill-for biscuit or puff quilts and other stuffed projects
Pillow inserts-for nicer looking pillows

BORDERS

Borders are added to quilted items for several different reasons. They are used to frame your quilt and to visually stop the quilt design from continuing into the borders. They increase the size of the quilt top. Borders also accent the center design.

Borders should be in scale with the rest of the quilt. It is best to add several narrow borders than to add just one wide border strip.

Borders may be square with the quilt or they may be mitered.

SQUARE BORDERS--

Sew border strips first to the two sides of the quilt. Press seam allowances away from quilt and toward the borders.
Sew border strips to top and bottom of quilt. Press seam allowances.

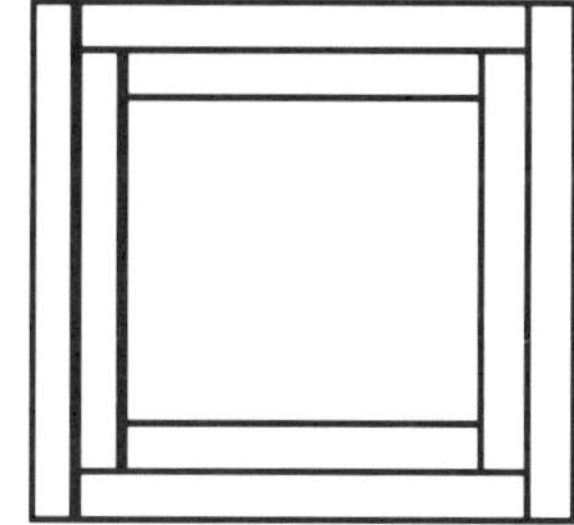

MITERED BORDERS--

Cut each border strip:

5" longer than the length of the side--if the borders are 2" wide.
7" longer than the length of the side--if the borders are 3" wide.

The border strips should extend past the edge of the quilt top and adjoining borders. Begin and end your sewing 1/4" in from the edge of the quilt top. Lock stitches by lowering the feed dogs, or set the stitch length on 0, and take several stitches.

Sew all four of the border strips to the quilt top. Make sure that all 4 strips are hanging loose at each end. Press all seam allowances toward the border strips.

Lay the borders in their finished position.
Overlap the extensions.
Trim the border extensions even with each other.

Bring two borders, right sides together.
Sew from the locked stitches on the quilt top out to the corner.
If necessary, mark your sewing line.
Trim the excess seam allowance.

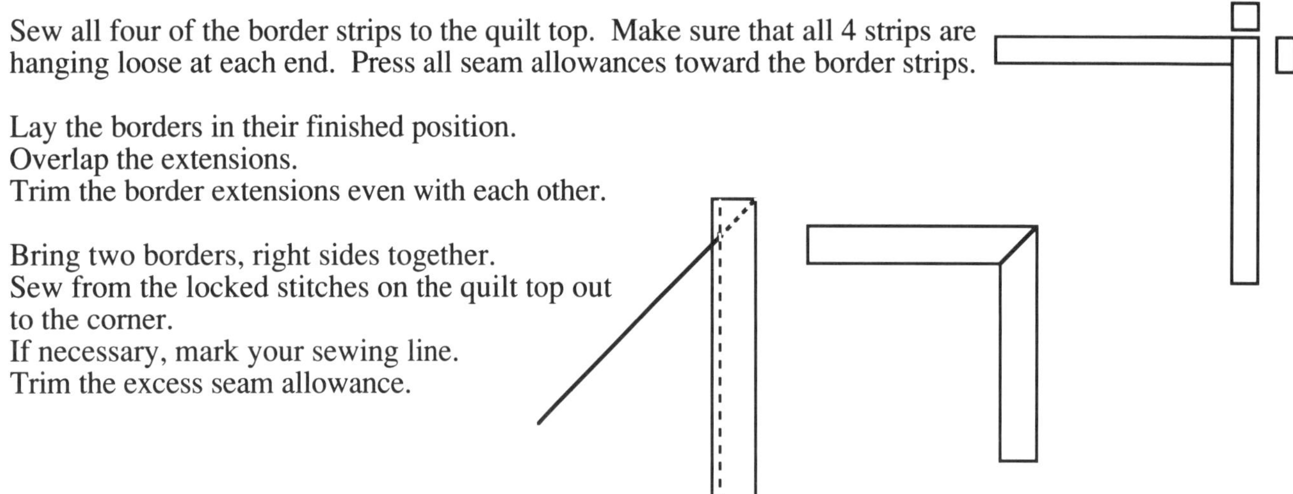

PRAIRIE POINTS

Strip-pieced prairie points save lots of time. There is no need to try to space them evenly around your quilt. They are already spaced and ready to go on your quilt.

The regular Prairie Points are found in "STRIP QUILTING PROJECTS". But try this variation--

PIPED PRAIRIE POINTS:

Place a piping strip between two strips of fabric (use a solid and a print or stripe), right sides together, the raw edge of the piping even with raw edges of the fabric.
Use a piping foot or a zipper foot and sew through both layers of fabric and piping.
Turn fabric right sides out.
Pin raw edges of fabric together and sew 1/2" from edge.

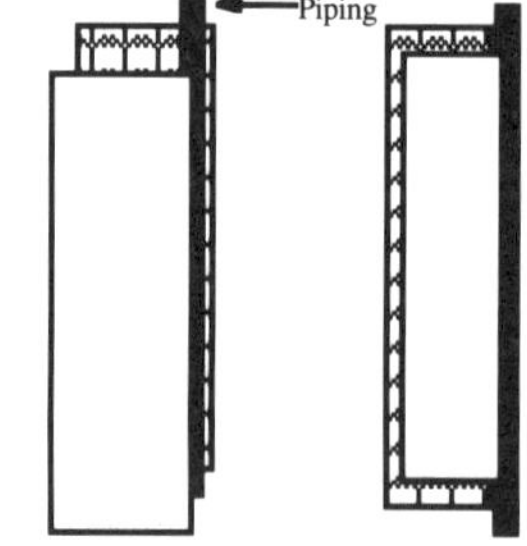

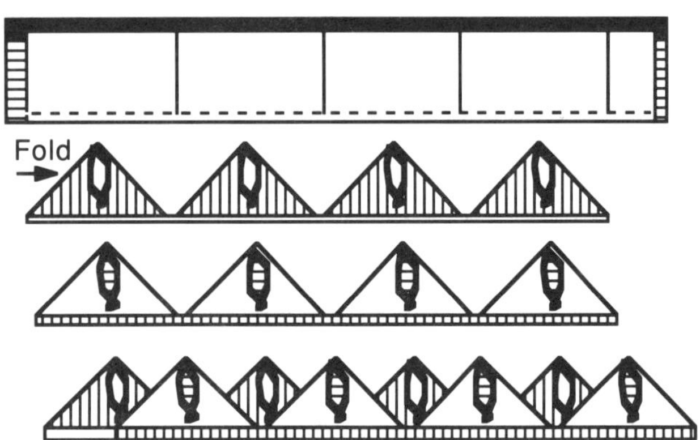

Measure the width of strip from this sewing line to top of piping strip. Double this measurement to cut the strip from piping just down to sewing line.

Fold both sides, of these cut edges, into the center, down to the sewing line. Fold with the print or stripe on the outside; or fold with the print or stripe on the inside, or fold some of each and combine them into an interesting finish.
Pin two prairie point strips together with points offset. Baste zigzag the raw edges to sewing line.

Place the prairie point strip, right sides together, with the quilt top.
The raw edges of the quilt even with raw edges of prairie points. Sew. Use an envelope style finish.

EYELET

Eyelet is sewn, right sides together, to three or four sides of the quilt top. It is more comfortable to sleep under a quilt that does not have eyelet at the top next to your face. The binding on the gathered part of the eyelet should be even with the edges of the quilt. For nice full corners, as you approach the corner, remove about 9" of the eyelet binding; run a row of machine basting stitches where the binding was removed. Gather the eyelet and sew around the corner. Finish with envelope style.

ENVELOPE FINISH

An envelope, or pillow case finish requires a backing fabric cut the same size as the quilt top. The two pieces are then sewn, right sides together, with or without batting. A binding is usually not used with this type of finish.

Sew around 3 1/2 sides of the quilt; If batting is sewn into the seam line, the batting should be next to the quilt top--this will eliminate the seam allowance showing through from the top of the quilt.

An envelope finish can be combined with piping, lace or eyelet.

QUILTING

LAYER YOUR QUILT

Tape, with basting tape, your backing, right side down, to a flat surface. Keep it taut, but don't stretch it. Place the batting on the backing. Place the quilt top, right side up, on the batting. Safety pin baste the three layers together (don't close the pins until all pins are inserted in the quilt--when you close the pins, you tend to lift up the backing). Use lots of pins--one on every side of every line you plan to quilt.

TIE YOUR QUILT BY MACHINE

Set your machine for sewing on buttons--a wide zigzag stitch; drop the feed dogs (or set your stitch length at 0). Your thread should match the color of the yarn or ribbon.
Tie the yarn or ribbon; lay it in place; take several zigzag stitches

To just bartack your quilt--set your machine as above; just zigzag without the yarn or ribbon.

MACHINE QUILTING

Bring bobbin thread through to top of quilt. Hold both bobbin and top thread. Start quilting by either dropping feed dogs and taking several stitches or shorten the stitch length to lock your stitches. Use matching thread or invisible (clear or smoke) thread in the needle. The bobbin thread should match the quilt backing. When turning corners, lock stitches to prevent a thread from pulling across the corner.
The stitch length is determined by the loft of the batting--lengthen if necessary. You may need to reduce the pressure on your presser foot.
Don't pull or push quilt through the machine.

STITCH IN DITCH-- Sew in seam line between strips.

FREE MOTION QUILTING--Remove your presser foot. If possible, place quilt in a machine embroidery hoop. If a hoop isn't possible, you will need an embroidery foot for your machine. Bring bobbin thread up through quilt. Hold both bobbin and needle thread. Don't turn your work--instead move it side to side, frontwards and backwards.

BINDINGS

A binding finishes off the edges and forms a frame around the quilt. Binding strips may be cut on the straight of grain or on the bias. If the edges of the quilt are straight, I prefer a straight cut binding; it is much easier to handle and takes much less fabric.

How wide should the binding be? The binding can be very narrow (1/8") to extra wide depending on the look you want on your quilt. If your finished binding (the width showing on the quilt top) is 1/2", then the seam allowance used to join the binding to the quilt must be 1/2" because the binding must be padded with the edge of the quilt.

Bindings may be made from a single layer strip, but a double-fold binding will lay smoother and last longer.

To cut a double binding,

cut the strips 6 times the desired finished width of the binding

How much binding do you need?

Add 2 x the length of the quilt + 2 x the width of the quilt plus 1 extra foot (just in case).

Fold the bias or straight binding in half lengthwise with the wrong sides together.
An easy way to do this is to use a long straight pin, an iron, and an ironing board:

Stick the long pin into the ironing board cover, up over the folded strip, and back into the ironing board. Place an iron to the right of the pin. Pull the strip under the pin and under the iron. It will come out folded and pressed perfectly.

MITERED BINDINGS

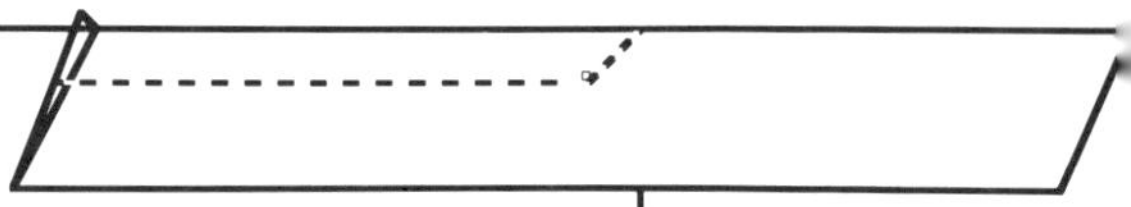

Start applying the binding on one side of the quilt--never at the corner. Leave a 6" tail at the beginning of the binding.
Sew with both raw edges of the binding even with the edge of the quilt.
At each corner of the quilt, stitch to a seam allowance width from the next edge.
With the needle in the quilt, pivot the quilt and sew to the corner.
(This will give you a perfect mitered corner on both the front and back of your quilt).

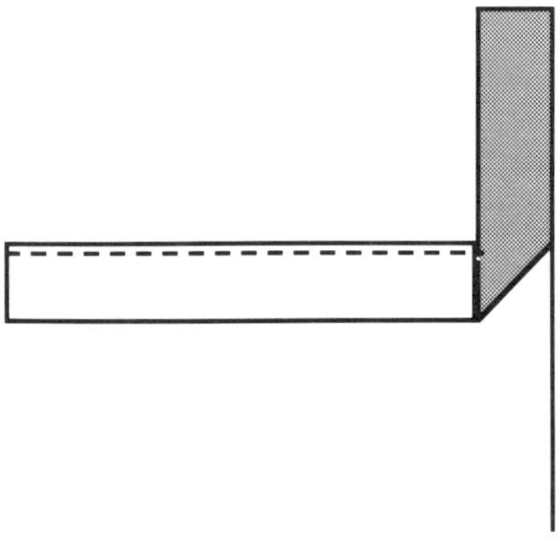

Fold the binding strip up at right angles.

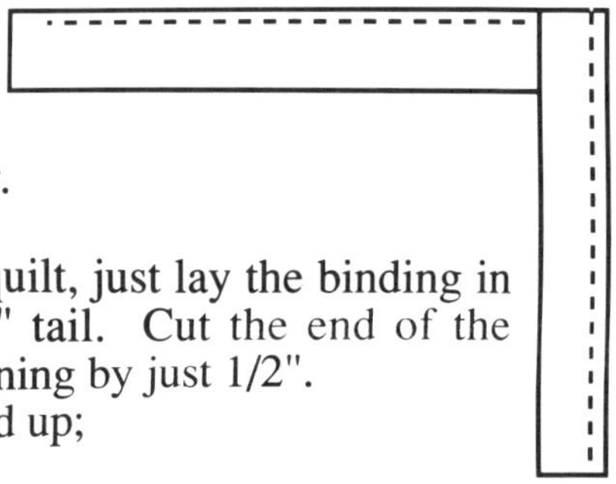

Bring the binding down square with the corner. (This forms a pleat.)

Sew from the edge to the next corner.

After turning the 4th corner of the quilt, just lay the binding in place overlapping the beginning 6" tail. Cut the end of the binding strip so it overlaps the beginning by just 1/2".
Bring the two ends of the binding strip, right sides together and opened up;
sew the ends together with 1/4" seam.
This will eliminate the bulky ending that you see on so many bindings.

FACED BINDINGS

Occasionally, I prefer not to have the binding show on the front of my quilt, such as when I use an interesting stripe for an outside border. Then I use a faced binding.

This is a single layer faced binding:
Cut strips 1 1/4" wide.
Sew strip, right sides together, with the quilt top.
On the back of quilt, line up raw edge of binding even with the seam line.
Then fold seam allowance and binding to back. Hand stitch in place.
The binding will only show on back of quilt.

HOW TO HANG YOUR QUILT

You can hang your quilt with hang tabs or with a sleeve on the back.

Hang tabs: Cut a 2" x 20" strip. Fold into thirds using iron and pin (see folding bindings). Top stitch close to both long edges. Cut the tab strip into 4 equal pieces. Sew the tabs evenly to the back of the quilt along the top edge. Finish with binding or use an envelope finish.

Sleeve: Cut a 5" strip the width of your quilt. Turn under the short ends and top stitch. Sew the top of the strip, wrong side of strip to back of quilt, even with top edge. This edge will be covered with the binding. Fold under the bottom of the strip and hand stitch in place.

FUSIBLE APPLIQUES

To make a fabric applique, use an Applique Pressing Sheet to fuse Stitch Witchery or Finefuse to the back of the fabric; cut out the applique; Lay in place on the backing fabric, cover with the Applique Pressing Sheet; press. Your applique is now fused and ready for a satin stitch (close zigzag).

IRONING PAD

On my television show, I use an ironing pad instead of an ironing board. You can make your own pad by layering these fabrics (cut to whatever size you desire, e.g., 24" x 24"):

cotton or sheeting
A layer of fleece or Thermore
a metallic coated fleece, such as an old ironing board cover
A layer of fleece or Thermore
cotton sheeting.

Zigzag (wide, long stitch) or serge all four edges.

SPECIAL OFFERS for YOU

5 QUILTING VIDEOS -- FEATURING KAYE WOOD

KV1 BASIC LOG CABIN
Step-by-step completed quilt
Mitered bindings
Pin basting
Machine quilting
Machine tying
From "Quilt Like A Pro", Chapter 6

KV2 REVERSIBLE QUILTS
Step-by-step
Unique 3-layer quilting
Sewing machine/sergers
Enclosed seams
Reversible vests
From "Turn Me Over--I'm Reversible

KV3 LOG CABIN TRIANGLES
Step-by-step
Easy triangle designs
Precision piecing
Unusual fabrics or "dogs"
From "Starmakers Ablaze I"

KV4 LOG CABIN DIAMONDS
Strip pieced diamonds
Four different sewing methods
Mitered hexagon borders
Precision piecing
Perfect points
Mitered bindings
From "Starmakers Ablaze II"

KV5 STARMAKER QUILT DESIGNS
Strip pieced quilts using the Starmaker tools for precision
Stars, Triangles, Diamonds, Dresden Plate designs
Perfect points
From all the STRIP LIKE A PRO Series books

T.V. SPECIAL---VIDEO TAPES 20% OFF the regular price of $29.95

To order video tapes

1. Send your name, address and phone number

2. We will send VHS tapes unless you specify Beta or European (PAL)

3. Send just $24.00 plus shipping for each video tape*
   Shipping & Handling -- Add 15% (maximum $5.00)
   IN & MI add sales tax
   Payment may be made by check, Visa/MC or COD
   For Visa/MC--
   include card number
   Expiration date
   and the name listed on the card.

*For European System (PAL) tapes only, the regular price is $39.95, the Special price is $34.00 plus shipping

KAYE WOOD PUBLISHING CO.
4949 Rau Road
West Branch, MI 48661
517-345-3028